FINALLY FREE

Let fear take you to your next adventure

Carol Foutz

First published by Ultimate World Publishing 2022
Copyright © 2022 Carol Foutz

ISBN

Paperback - 978-1-922714-69-5
Ebook - 978-1-922714-70-1

Carol Foutz has asserted her right under the Copyright, Designs and Patents Act 1988 to be identified as the author of this work. The information in this book is based on the author's experiences and opinions. The publisher specifically disclaims responsibility for any adverse consequences, which may result from use of the information contained herein. Permission to use information has been sought by the author. Any breaches will be rectified in further editions of the book.

All rights reserved. No part of this publication may be reproduced, stored in or introduced into a retrieval system, or transmitted in any form, or by any means (electronic, mechanical, photocopying, recording or otherwise) without the prior written permission of the author. Any person who does any unauthorised act in relation to this publication may be liable to criminal prosecution and civil claims for damages. Enquiries should be made through the publisher.

Cover design: Ultimate World Publishing
Layout and typesetting: Ultimate World Publishing
Editor: James Salmon

Ultimate World Publishing
Diamond Creek,
Victoria Australia 3089
www.writeabook.com.au

Testimonials

"Brazen, Energetic, and Courageous...Definitely not your Momma's self-help book." A life journey that details the denial, lies, excuses, attitudes, and daily struggles of alcohol addiction. A provocative exposé of the multiple attempts and failures that are suffered before reaching and maintaining a sober existence. This story exposes the reader to life-shattering experiences and barriers that make recovery an almost impossible undertaking.

Martin A. Martinez

Carol is my best friend and my mother. I cannot begin to write the words to explain how proud I am of her for sharing her story. I myself have a one-year-old girl and what I have learned as an adult and now parent is, as our parents raise us, we think they have it all figured out and know all things. I now see that they are just humans trying to keep it all together and figure this insane life out. Now I am reading my mom's story and seeing just how much life she had to figure out. Her words will inspire others to be self-reflective, self-forgiving, and self-persevering. This is a story that many people can relate to but not many people experience all in one lifetime. It does however explain why she is so incredible.

Dakota Rae Kennedy

Finally Free

One woman's tale of resilience, faith and recovery. An uplifting story that will resonate with those who have struggled, both in and out of addiction. Honest and fearless... humorous and heart-warming.

Anne-Marie Bebber

Carol's story is one of hardship, perseverance and remaining true to oneself in the face of adversity, and her voice is present throughout what is a compelling read. Her unique writing style makes her an engaging storyteller, transporting the reader into what is an enthralling journey. Whether you're looking for inspiration, entertainment, or something else entirely, Carol's is a story worth reading.

Regards,
James

Contents

Testimonials	iii
Dedication	vii
Introduction	1
My Mom's Story	3
My Story	19
Afterword	209
About the Author	211
Speaker Bio	213

Dedication

This book is dedicated to my mom, Mel and my daughter. You have both been the driving force in my life for good and an inspiration to continue helping others and believing in myself. I love you with all of who I am and my hope is that you will continue to see me the way I see you.

Introduction

I have been told through the years that I should write a book about my life. I did not think it was interesting enough to write an actual book, until now. This book is a journey through my life as a child, young adult, woman, mother, and recovering alcoholic discovering who I truly want to be through some really good and bad choices.

I had no idea how difficult this would be putting into print the things that I tucked away for so long and the freedom this process would give me. My hope is to inspire others to find their strengths in every situation and know that our struggles are only opportunities for growth. Helping others through their challenges with compassion is the most important act of kindness.

My Mom's Story

Chapter 1

It was 1967 and I was like any other teen ager, until 1968. My mother was a physical education teacher, my father an entrepreneur. What I mean by entrepreneur is that he never held a job, but appeared to always be working. His greatest skills were getting people to listen to him and being a friend. He played Santa Claus on television one year at a local station. He was 6'3" and had a beautiful white beard. His smile was captivating. When he spoke, you wanted to believe every word, as the feeling of promise and hope filled your entire body. He was going places for sure.

My mother's smile was also captivating. However, it appeared to diminish when she looked my way. It was more of a disappointing glare when our eyes met. My mother stood five-feet-tall and was a beautiful woman. Her hair was always in place and she had the straightest back and large breasts. Back then, bras were pointed,

Finally Free

as if to direct women which way to go. She was very stern and never a rule-breaker. She taught physical education for high school kids and was very structured. She did have a sense of humor but I rarely saw it. My parents were total opposites in every way. I soon learned I would need to maneuver my way through this life as the pride and joy of one and the regret of the other.

I was pretty enough, I guess. I had long black hair, blue eyes and was very fit. I lived in Southern California, where the culture itself promotes an active lifestyle. I had a passion for dancing and partying with my best friends, Lindsey, Rebecca, Christine and Darlene. My mom had a felt picture of me in her home up until the day she died. I am not sure if she was proud, or dancing was the one thing I did well. I was always finding reasons to leave my house, and my friends often had ideas of what we could do. I wanted to please my mother but I truly did not know how. It was easier to stay out of her way.

My father and I spent time together, visiting his friends and talking to strangers on the street. There was one last stop before returning home – the bar. He was quite a drinker. I was too young to drink but I would jump up on the bar stool and the bartender would have a Shirley Temple waiting for me: sprite, red juice and a cherry. I don't recall having to drive him around due to his drinking but I do remember running to my room before my mother started talking to him in her disappointed tone. I really didn't ever blame her. It must have been very hard to be with someone so free when she herself was in a prison of expectations.

My Mom's Story

Chapter 2

My friends and I were considered a popular group of girls. There were always boys around us and we were invited to all the cool parties. We were friends with all kids and didn't have any drama within our group. I was not as confident as my friends but, with a little alcohol, it was easier for me to pretend I was. Still, on the inside, I was just so lonely; seeking love that I didn't have to work for, from a person who had no expectations of me.

I had another friend outside of my friend group. Her name was Carol. She was from a Catholic family. They appeared to be so put together, with so much love in their home. She had many brothers and sisters and there was always something fun happening at their house. One of Carol's brothers was Paul. He was very handsome and we liked each other. We secretly dated on and off. Basically, we had sex from time to time, no strings attached. We knew this could never be a real relationship – after all, I wasn't Catholic.

Finally Free

When Paul and I were "off", I met another boy named Bill. We met at a bar. He was super fun and very kind. I went to his house that night and saw a picture of his mother. His mother was the first lady to sit in a martini glass. You may have to do some research to understand what that means. We had sex one time, then Bill moved away. I never saw him again. Though our encounter was brief, it would change the direction of my life. I was about to find the love I had been seeking for so long. It was just different than I had expected.

Nine months later, I found myself sitting in a room, waiting to sign adoption papers for my unborn child. My mind was spinning out of control. I couldn't believe I was in this situation, again. I had gotten pregnant and had had to get an abortion before. This action was not my choice. My father drove me to Mexico to terminate the pregnancy. I don't recall if I ever told my mother. It was horrible. I knew right then, I would never be the same person I was prior to entering that dark place, in a city I had never been to, with a doctor I was not even sure was actually a doctor. I told myself at that moment, this would never happen again. Well, part of this never did happen again.

Do I sign the papers, or keep my baby?

Chapter 3

I left the adoption agency feeling a sense of relief. I drove to my friend's party that had been taking place while I was making the biggest decision of my life. When I walked in the house, the girls eagerly ran to my side. They offered their condolences and support for this poor girl, who they thought had signed away her unborn child, to a family she would never know. I said to my friends, "I just couldn't do it, I'm keeping her". We all screamed, "We're having a baby!"

Lindsey, Rebecca, Christine and Darlene wanted the baby to have their names. However, when I saw my baby, Carol was the name I chose. This would be the love that would continue to fill my soul, and the souls of my mother and father. The only problem was, "Who is the father?"

Paul and I agreed not to tell anyone that he may be the father. I was only with Bill one time and I truly believed my baby was Paul's.

Finally Free

Carol became the secret, and she belonged to me. Lindsey, Rebecca, Christine, Darlene and I had to figure out a last name for my baby. It never crossed my mind to give her my last name. We needed a fictitious man, who would be named on her birth certificate.

We came up with the name Ronald A. Walker. I had seen "Johnny Walker" on a billboard many times driving to and from school. Yes, Johnny Walker, the liquor. I was 19 and not very creative. We discussed different careers Ronald should have. A mechanic seemed the most reasonable: not too fancy, but definitely important. Of course, he was in the Army. It was the 60s, so that was a no-brainer. I wonder now if we should have planned to kill him off; that way, it would make sense that he was never around. Here she was, Carol Lynn Walker.

Two years later, I had another child, this time a boy. I knew who his father was this time. I had learned my lesson. He had no interest in building a family with me but he did show love to the three of us. He came around from time to time but slowly disappeared into his own life and I moved on with mine. It wasn't even a question in my mind that everything would be okay. As long as I worked hard and was a good person it would all work out.

After all, I had the support of my parents. "You can imagine how excited my mother was." I was now 21 with two beautiful children, who my parents loved as if they were their own. They basically raised them, but the kids always knew I was their mom, and that I loved them. I worked for Pacific Bell and this made it hard for me to spend a lot of time with them. Besides, I was very young, so I needed time with my friends.

My Mom's Story

Carol was nine when I met my first and only husband. He worked with me at the phone company and appeared to have his life in order. He also had two kids of his own part time. Would this be the one?

Chapter 4

Tom whisked me off my feet and moved us to New Mexico. Okay, it wasn't actually a whisk. He promised the world, and delivered nothing – well almost. I was now in a relationship I was not ready for and in a town I didn't know. But I was determined to make this work, and give my kids a real home and a complete family. Together, I would have another son.

One day, I took the kids skiing in Durango, Colorado. It was a ski resort, close to the town we moved to, in New Mexico. It was a beautiful, warm, sunny day. My son and I were at the bottom of the mountain, Carol, at the top. Carol tended to go her own way. She had no problem being alone. She absolutely loved her brother, and would do anything for him. She skied down the mountain to get him for the next run. I watched them jump on the lift, and up they went. I had no idea what would come back down that beautiful mountain.

Finally Free

I was in the ski lodge, enjoying my time alone. Suddenly, the door flew open. Carol was standing there with this look on her face that I will never forget. She was so angry. Earlier, for some unknown reason, I told my son that he and Carol are half brother and sister. When he and Carol were on the chair lift, Carol said something, which encouraged him to say, "You're just my half-sister". I realized at that moment that giving them the same, fake last name was not going to be enough. I quickly told Carol that her dad was Paul. Carol loved Paul and she knew she was named after his sister. She was happy about the new information and I was forgiven. "Wow, that wasn't so bad," I thought. "This will never be brought up again." Until it was.

Through the years, Carol would ask questions about Paul and me. I had to admit to my own daughter that there may be a chance that her biological father was not Paul. Since Carol was in her 20s by this time, she was more understanding than I could have imagined. I contacted Paul. He agreed to a DNA test. Carol and Paul waited eagerly for the results. Paul called and delivered the news. Carol got tears in her eyes and Paul said, "Carol, I really wish it would have been me". Carol offered to pay him back the 200 bucks for the test, which of course he declined. The next phone call would be more difficult since I had not spoken to Bill in over 20 years and had no idea how to find him.

I found a phone number through information (411). I called and told Bill the story. Carol then called Bill. He was very receptive in the beginning. He told Carol he loved her. He was sorry he didn't know about her sooner. He asked if they could talk again after the holidays. He needed some time to tell his wife. Carol was now 30-something. Unfortunately, Bill's wife was not interested in any of this.

My Mom's Story

Bill sent Carol a Christmas ornament that year with a picture of his face. Soon after, Carol got the news that he would not go further in building a relationship or doing a DNA test, due to his wife having MS. The ornament was quickly smashed on the small concrete patio outside the apartment where Carol and her daughter lived. Years later, Carol found her half-sister online, and she agreed to do a DNA test. Bill was the father. Her half-sister was only three months younger. Her mother arrived on Bill's doorstep with her when she was four years old. Bill's wife was not about to have this happen to her again.

Chapter 5

Carol would become a single mother, like me. She would learn from my mistakes, and do things differently. Still, she would struggle to find love in a man who would stand by her, encourage her to be herself, and care for her child alongside her. Though the apple doesn't fall far from the tree, it still falls.

As I sat in my trailer thinking about the past and how different things could have been, I got so depressed I could hardly move. I was not a grandma that is seen on tv. I didn't knit sweaters or bake homemade cookies. I didn't connect to who I was or who I was supposed to be. When I was deep in self-pity, the phone would ring, and it would be one of my kids. I would hear in their voice a part of something I did that was so right, it can't be denied.

I brought three amazing humans into the world. I held my mother's hand as she was taking her last breath. I saw the love she had for me in her eyes. I took care of my father as he died from diabetes

Finally Free

in my living room due to his alcoholism. I moved to a new town, with much internal despair, but with hope of providing a childhood for my kids that I had only ever dreamed about.

I found a part of myself through a 12-step program and for a while I was truly free. I rid myself of negative people and behaviors that were cancerous in my life which in part left me isolated and alone. As the cancers slowly returned through the years, I realized, I still had time to keep removing the barriers to my happiness. I had a desire to remember the remarkable things that I have done and the experiences I have had, and the people who not only have I loved, but who have loved me. I remember the time when I considered naming my baby, Lindsey Rebecca Christine Darlene. Now, if I could just get my 34-year-old son to move out of my trailer.

My Story

Chapter 6

Up to this point, you, the reader, have experienced my mom's story through my eyes. I don't remember as a child feeling anything but love for my mom. I knew she loved me and was truly doing the best she could. We lived in Los Angeles until I was nine years old. She worked for the telephone company and it was very far from our home. We had to be woken up at 4 am, due to LA traffic. She would throw some clothes in a paper bag and wrap a blanket around us. We had the pajamas with the feet so we were always warm enough. Mom had to drop us off at the babysitters, sometimes people we knew, sometimes perfect strangers. One time my mom picked us up and the sitter was nowhere in sight. I told my mom she had gone to the store. My mom waited for her to come back and let her have it pretty good. We never went back to that one. There was one place where all the potty chairs were lined up against the house out back. We didn't stay there either.

Finally Free

My mom had really good friends during and after high school but they all started going their own way. One of my favorite stories is of me and my friend Stephanie playing in the closet at Stephanie's house. We were putting on her mom's high heels and making clicking noises on the wood floors. Her mom's name was Stephanie as well. The moms were talking in the kitchen about how people would give Stephanie Sr. a hard time about Stephanie Jr. being black, since Stephanie Sr. was white. We heard this and ran over to our moms. I said, with an inquisitive and confused tone, "Stephanie's black?" Stephanie Jr. said "I'm black?" They just started laughing and me and Stephanie went back to playing. We wonder when kids find the differences – that was my moment. I was seven years old.

We were always moving from place to place, finding the cheapest rent or getting us closer to the job. We stayed with my grandparents many times in between. Mom moved us out of my grandparents' home and into an apartment with a dolphin on the outside. This was a really fun time for me. I had a lot of friends in the complex and we rode our plastic three-wheelers back and forth on the white concrete deck upstairs. Once there was an earthquake and my younger brother was going up the stairs and was wearing those leg braces because he was pigeon-toed. My mom scooped him up the stairs as small cracks were appearing in the stairs. I saw the strength in my mom that day and she was like a superhero. She never has seen that in herself, but hopefully one day she will.

My brother and I went to a school fair and we each won a goldfish. When we came home a few days later one of the goldfish had died. They were identical but I told him how sorry I was that his goldfish died. I was compassionate, but also manipulative, I guess.

My Story

Our meals consisted of TV dinners. Not the good kind they have today. We had the ones with that disgusting "Chocolate Cake" and the mashed potatoes that came out in one scoop. It was fun opening up the tin foil and being surprised about what the meal was for the evening. I tried not to look at the picture on the box to make it fun. We always got to eat in front of the TV. This was a family tradition that would continue throughout my life.

After the last babysitter incident, Mom found a more responsible and safer place for us to go while she was working and playing. The couple she left us with were named Aunt Judy and Uncle George. In the living room stood a large elephant made out of dark wood and one baby elephant on each side of the mom. Many times, we slept over at Aunt Judy's, due to my mom staying out so late. Aunt Judy said that if we got up in the middle of the night the elephants would walk the rooms, and she would know. I never did get out of that bed until the morning came.

Aunt Judy stood about 5'2" and very round. She had long black hair which she kept in a tight bun and false teeth. She was very firm but fair. Many children came in and out of her home with very different backgrounds. Aunt Judy appeared much older than her husband George. He was freer and more easygoing. He was very fit, tan, and so handsome, like a movie star from the 50s. They were an interesting couple. Aunt Judy bossed him around pretty good and he would just smile and do the next requested chore.

Uncle George was in construction and had built a large pool with a slide in the backyard. There was an adult-sized dollhouse out back across from the pool. He had built that for the one daughter of their own, but she was grown by the time we started going there. No one was allowed in the dollhouse. At least, not until the day that we were told my mom was in New Mexico and had married a man who we had only met once. From that day on I was allowed to play in the dollhouse and got to sleep in a bedroom with a door so I didn't have to worry about the elephants at night.

I found out about my mom's new marriage when I had come inside the house to dry off for lunch. I was standing next to the washer and dryer, which was running most of the time. Aunt Judy said she had something to tell me. I had asked her earlier when my mom was going to be coming to pick us up, so she was giving me an update. Aunt Judy said, "Your mom got married and she is in New Mexico." Just a reminder, I was in Los Angeles. I asked, "To who?" She gave his name, but I really didn't hear it. I quickly ran back to the pool and continued playing. This may have been the beginning of learning what the feeling of abandonment is and not knowing what to do with it.

Chapter 7

A few weeks later, my mom sent for us through my grandma. My Aunt Veronica, who was married to my mom's brother, and my grandma, loaded up the maroon Malibu and drove us to New Mexico. The house we would now be living in was a beautiful two-story house that was painted "Smurf" blue. Mom's new husband, Tom, drove one of those 80s vans with a beach scene on the sliding side door. He had black curly hair like he had gotten a perm and seemed nice enough. He owned two bowling alleys, we were never without the opportunity to work.

This is where my childhood would be full of amazing friendships, trauma, and exciting and disturbing events. Where innocence flourished and fears were revealed. Our house was located in a great community. We stayed out after dark riding bikes and had sleepovers without any fears. Our backyard was connected to the park and when it was dinner time my mom's husband would whistle to get us home. The grade school was within walking distance and I had plenty of friends to walk with to and from school.

My parents didn't go to church so I found a family that would take me. They had so many kids it was like I was just another one of theirs. They actually drove a large van and every Sunday I would walk over early so I could be a part of the chaos of getting so many kids ready for church. My house was pretty empty most of the time. My parents were always at the bowling alley so I pretty much had the run of the place.

Although church was something I always wanted to attend, there was a part of me that never felt like I belonged. This feeling would continue throughout my life. The families at church appeared more put together and loving, and really talked to and supported each other. Later I would learn this is not the truth and many families have their own little secrets and struggles. I had two alcoholic parents who didn't check my homework or take an interest in showing up for the sports I played in school. It wasn't until I read my journal as an adult that I saw how truly sad and alone I must have felt at times. Maybe writing in the journal allowed me to let the bad feelings go, through the words from pen to paper. Becoming more knowledgeable of my past as I grew up could have diminished a very happy childhood if I let it. In my mind I was very happy and wanted to make sure others around me were happy too. I had no idea there were secrets I was keeping. No one asked, so I had nothing to tell.

My grandma's name was Hazel and she died just before her 97th birthday. My grandpa was Richard but everyone called him Tex. I don't remember a time in my life prior to their death when they were too far away from me. My grandma was a very healthy, strong, smart, active and proud woman. She made sure I worked out at the pool and would sneak us in late at night to the adult pool so we could swim laps and play. She also taught me how to play tennis and shoot baskets. She didn't want to hear complaining; she wanted to know what the bottom line was, how she could help, and let's get it done. Since she was a PE teacher, that is what I was determined to be. I told her I didn't have to go to college. I would just wait until they needed teachers really badly and I would just get a job. She convinced me that wasn't going to happen. My grandma taught me the importance of living within your means and did not believe in credit cards. To this day I have never had a debt I couldn't pay.

My grandpa was my best friend. I went everywhere with him. He took me horseback riding one time and I got bucked off the horse and landed in manure. We laughed so hard he almost peed his pants. He did that a lot actually. Once we were on the Zipper at a local amusement park called Uncle Babe's. I kept sliding into him really hard as the Zipper twisted and turned, slamming me into his hip. He yelled, "Carol Lynn, you're going to make me pee my pants". He was from Texas so he had a bit of an accent.

My grandparents had those red and white encyclopedias, sold by the door-to-door sales person. There were some pages that had clear plastic over the skeletons of humans and each plastic page that could be lifted would show a little more of the internal body. When I opened those up while sitting on his lap, he would turn his head away and make a sound to show it was so gross he couldn't look at it. This would make me laugh hysterically.

Finally Free

Because my grandparents were so present in our lives, they too would eventually make the move to New Mexico. I would discover here that my grandpa was an alcoholic and my grandma would find one more husband after his passing. Once I was coming over for a visit and my grandpa was lying in the driveway with his face in the dirt in the middle of the day. I thought for sure he was dead. My mom and grandma rolled him over and helped him into the house. I don't recall any discussion on this matter. Another time he was drinking a glass of milk and dipping his toast into the glass. His eyes were droopy and his speech was weird. I was around ten. He started chewing on his fingers as if he was still eating the toast but the toast was no longer there. He had diabetes as well so my grandma said he just needed his shot. Those were the only two incidents that I remember making me feel very sad for him and not knowing what an alcoholic was and that he had a disease.

Before my grandparents moved near us, we were getting adjusted to our new lives in this small town in New Mexico. The two-story house had plenty of room for all of us. My mom's husband had a couple kids that would come visit. It was so much fun when they came to town. We did more activities, ate out at nice places and took "family" vacations. He was nicer and didn't drink as much when his kids were visiting. We didn't have any living room furniture the first couple of years. So, we all laid with blankets in front of the TV. Sometimes we would fall asleep.

Chapter 8

One evening I was wearing pajama shorts and a tank top. It was a matching set, purple with ruffles on the straps. I hated ruffles but our house was pretty hot in the summer and really cold in the winter. We fell asleep on the floor the night I was given my first secret. As I slept, I felt this wet feeling in the top crack of my butt. I jumped up and realized it was my stepfather's tongue. I walked over to the wall and just looked at him as I was half asleep. He motioned for me to come and said, "Come lay back down". I quickly went into my bedroom and jumped into my canopy bed. I told my stepsister, she said, "You're okay now, just go to sleep". And that is what I did.

I never had another thought about the incident until I was older and working with youth that had had their own experiences. However, it may have influenced my behavior with boys. I was the opposite of promiscuous. I wanted to be one of the boys, and I didn't want them to like me "like that," but I was definitely boy crazy. The good part of this is that I stayed a virgin all through high school. The bad part is that when I did finally have sex, I quickly learned I had a commodity that I could use to manipulate men. But let's not jump too far ahead. There is more family drama to uncover before we move into my 20s.

Like I mentioned, Tom owned two bowling alleys. I started off babysitting in the nursery then moved up to working the front desk. My brother learned to be the "Pin Boy". Tom was easily jealous of the relationship between my mom, brother and me. He would be cruel and make fun of us any chance he got, which is probably where I learned my sarcasm. Only once do I remember him being physical toward my little brother. We were all walking into the smaller bowling alley and my brother made a funny comment. Tom kicked him in the ass so hard his feet came off of the ground. Tom tried to make it a joke but I knew he meant it, especially when he was drinking. He wasn't a tough guy. He was a charmer. The smell of Gallo wine on his breath lingered in my memory into adulthood.

On the days he had not been drinking it could appear we were a really happy family, working together to operate this family business. Christmas was fun at his parents' place. They had a huge lawn and all the cousins came and we played football until dinner time. I have heard other families talk about the uncle who does the reach around on girls and touches the side boob. There was one of those there too but he wasn't an uncle. Luckily, I didn't have any boobs for a long time but sure enough when they came in it only took one time for me, and those hugs no longer happened.

Family vacations mostly consisted of going to other cities for bowling tournaments. Once Tom took us on a family vacation and left us

My Story

in the middle of it to fly home, to the woman he was having an affair with. Me, mom and my brother spent a bunch of money at Elvis Presley's house on ridiculous souvenirs. I got the blue slippers with Elvis heads on them. Sure, I wish I would have kept them; they would have been worth a lot of money today. Needless to say, "family vacations," for me, were fun in the beginning, then sad at the end. One time my stepbrother and I were getting into the van to take a trip and Tom threatened to throw a glass of wine on us. My stepbrother said, "I dare you," and Tom threw it. I guess I could say that was my first taste of alcohol. There were some really fun times, I have to admit, like holidays, and playing hide and seek at the bowling alley and at home. One time when we were playing hide and seek, my stepbrother hid under a couch downstairs, and we didn't find him for so long that when he finally came out, he was dripping sweat. Tom also let us hang our legs outside of the van when he was driving around the neighborhood. He did say not to fall out, because my mom would never believe it was an accident.

Chapter 9

I got really good at turning negatives into positives and making things fun with whatever the situation. Maybe it was a defense mechanism or maybe I was just a really happy person who had some bad things happen. Either way, my grade school and junior high years were awesome. I got my real first boyfriend in 6th grade, as real as that could be. His name was Leroy. He had curly black hair and brown eyes. He was very strong and played basketball. My friend Kaylee convinced me to do cheerleading, so I was able to cheer for his games. I hated wearing the uniform: striped gold and white long sleeve turtlenecks with a big royal blue B sewn on the front, blue skirts, and the worst were the blue bloomers. The best thing about the uniform were the shoes and the little balls on our laces. Of course, now that I am older, I wish I still had that little uniform as a reminder of an amazing part of my school days.

We were playing football on the playground during recess one day when Leroy accidentally threw a rock and it hit me. He felt so bad he

Finally Free

wouldn't come into the classroom after recess. The teacher asked me to go outside and get him back into class. I walked across our dirt playground with my light blue shirt that said, "Anything boys can do girls can do better." I truly believed that but would later learn that it is not always the case due to physical differences as well as other things.

Junior high brought new opportunities: sports, boys, meaner teachers, harder school work and many different friend groups. I was still involved in church and riding with the same family. One morning we were driving to church and my friend said something that I thought was very funny. Her dad reached around from the driver's seat and hit her in the leg. I thought to myself, I don't think you're supposed to do that on your way to church. I looked at him differently from that day forward.

Life was going so well and nothing could have changed the fun adventures I was experiencing. But then, my grandpa died. I was sitting in class at Heights Junior High School. I was 15 years old and Mr. Andrews, the principal, called me to the office. He looked very sad and he told me that he would do whatever he could to help me get through this. He also told me what a great guy my grandpa was and that felt really good. At that moment I no longer wanted to learn, I just wanted to have fun and do the bare minimum of class work. There was no one at home to talk me out of this, so my studies suffered and my social life got bigger and bigger.

Chapter 10

High school was a game-changer for sure. Due to my lack of interest in boys sexually, having my first drink would become the emotional adjustment I didn't know I was looking for. Boys caused a lot of drama with my friends. I saw more tears in high school than in the rest of my life to now. They complained about how their boyfriend or girlfriend slept with someone else and the next day they were back with them. I was not going to learn how to be a girlfriend in that place, that's for sure.

I was really excited to have my driver's license. I was now able to pick my parents up from the bowling alley at two in the morning because they were too drunk to drive. One time I was driving my mom home and she was very angry at Tom. Just before we made the turn to our street, she reached over and slammed the car into park. I remember thinking, I am never going to be like that when I drink. This was one of two times I ever saw my mom that angry. Though my mom made mistakes, she was an amazing and kind person. She just didn't do well when she drank alcohol. She would soon get sober right when my drinking began.

My mom became a member of a 12-step recovery program when I was 16. I never saw her so happy. She divorced Tom, had solid friendships, and was so beautiful and energetic. She was very fit and had a great body to match her outgoing personality. The person she was on the outside finally matched how I saw her on the inside. She continued to work a lot but that's what she was passionate about. She also worked with other women in recovery. One time she took us to a meeting with her. The room was full of smoke and bearded men who were very emotional. It was such a weird thing to realize that this room was what got her to this happiness. They were always having activities, and everyone was talking to each other, hugging and laughing. The downside was I felt that I was being left behind. The house became emptier and I was entering a new world of teenagers with freedom, cars and alcohol.

We had an away basketball game in Newcomb. It was a dusty little town in the desert. We had to take a bus there and would be returning home when it was dark. Two of my friends and I were waiting in the parking lot for the bus. A couple of boys came up to us and offered us some Southern Comfort. I was definitely not afraid of a challenge but I wasn't sure if this was a good choice. It took some convincing from my friends because they had drunk alcohol before this night. Down it went. I remember how warm it was but it didn't seem to do anything except make us laugh a lot. It is true that the only way to keep a secret is to never tell anyone. Well, we got told on and kicked off the basketball team.

My Story

I was super embarrassed but didn't mind too much because I never liked basketball. Arm pits in your face during a time when not all girls shaved, and running back and forth were tough with my asthma. I don't recall the second time I drank alcohol – it just became a thing that we did on the weekends. We went out to the hills and the bluffs with a keg and the solo cups. I realized very quickly I was pretty good at drinking and that's when my best counseling came out. There was always someone having an issue with someone else who loved to talk to me about it, and I liked giving them advice. I made it through high school a virgin, but that was more based on fear than anything else. I don't even remember being curious. I just liked kissing and holding hands and that was all I needed.

Chapter 11

At 19, I met my first husband. Let's call him Steve for the purpose of this story. Steve was super athletic, very strong, had an excellent physique, and was very popular with the girls. He wasn't much of a conversationalist, which I didn't mind, because I talked enough for both of us. We saw each other at the gym through the years, so it was easy for us to talk about going to a party together. He had really good-looking friends, so of course I made friends with their female friends.

On our first trip out to the hills we were driving in his huge lifted truck with dirt flying behind us and rocks getting shot into the windshield from the car in front of us. I was so excited to be a part of this adventure. Steve looked over and said, "Put out or get out", as he slowed the truck down to a stop. I said, "No problem", and quickly jumped out of the truck and started walking back toward the paved road. Steve threw the truck in reverse and said he was only kidding. I knew then this commodity was very powerful. Now I just had to figure out how I was supposed to use it and whether it would help me or destroy me.

Steve and I dated for quite some time. One day I was driving in front of his house to drop him off and there was a flood, so he had to help me get my El Camino out. As I drove off, he yelled, "I love you!" I looked at my friend who was in the car and started freaking out. "Did you hear that?" She yelled, "YES!" So, I yelled back out the window, "I love you too!" I didn't know if I loved him or not, but I knew it felt nice to hear, and it was pretty cool to say.

While this crazy relationship was happening, I was also on my way to college in Las Cruces with my friend Donna. Donna and her family were like a second family to me. She lived outside of town and her family had a large property where we rode horses and dirt bikes. They also had a really cute stable boy. He was actually much older but super nice. Donna's parents were older, and Donna was very mature for her age. She had her own car, and we had been friends since grade school. I loved staying the night at her house. She would make the carnation instant breakfast for me in the morning and they had the coolest cups. I liked watching her put her makeup on but I never really got into it. It seemed like a lot of work and when I did try it just didn't look good. My mom wasn't into make-up either. She was naturally pretty.

Donna and I were pretty different as far as economic status, but she was real and wasn't afraid to say what was on her mind. We were both pretty much down for anything. In fact, I wouldn't have even considered college if it wasn't for her. I lasted about a month or two and she left shortly after. I had no idea what I was doing in college. We lived on campus and had some girl telling us how to clean the toilet and no boys were allowed in our room. This was only day one. So of course, the first thing we did was invite Steve and our friend Eugene to Las Cruces for the weekend. I didn't even know I had a counselor to help me choose the classes, so I just picked what I thought looked fun. One day it had been raining and I was riding my bike across campus trying to find a class. My tires slipped and I slid across the pavement in front of a bunch of people. It was the weirdest thing; everyone just continued about not paying any attention.

During the visit with the boys, we went to Tijuana. Steve was driving because he wasn't a drinker. He had never driven on a freeway. He saw our exit to the right across the median and drove over the median, which lead to the same lane we were in before. We all started laughing so hard because he didn't realize he could just drive a little further to be on the same lane we were in.

My drinking started to get more frequent, and I felt like I was making decisions so quickly I didn't even know what I was doing. I left school just after that visit from the boys because Steve asked me to marry him. All three of our rings cost $400 and I thought they were the most beautiful rings in the world.

When Steve asked me to marry him, I was hesitant due to him being a mechanic. I mean after all, the fake guy on my birth certificate was a mechanic and that didn't work out so well. So, I told him if he joined the Marine Corp, I would marry him. My brother had signed up and I totally respect the military. In my mind this would give us some security; he would fight for our country and I would work in the schools as a P.E. teacher. I also wanted to get back to California and this was a great way to do it.

I knew Steve was the one to marry because of two bicycle accidents. When I returned home from a family trip, I was at a stop light, and here comes Steve on his bicycle to meet me. As he was coming toward me a car hit him and he flew off of his bike and landed in the windshield of the guy's car. He rolled to the ground, stood up, then went up to the guy, grabbed his shirt, and started yelling at him. I ran toward Steve and told him we had to go to the hospital because his head was cut open. We threw his bike in the back of my El Camino and went to the emergency room.

At the emergency room, Steve gave false information on the paperwork because he didn't have any money to pay for treatment. This was uncomfortable but as long as I wasn't talking, I wasn't lying. I thought about the time I stole Smurfs with my friends. What a weird thing to steal. I actually got caught and the guy told my mom it seemed like I was trying to get caught. Me and my friends had actually stolen so many we each had a collection at our houses. I took all of mine back and my mom paid for them. I didn't like the adrenaline rush breaking the law gave me. I was no angel but I did know right from wrong, and wrong was very uncomfortable. Steve got his stitches and off to work he went.

The second bike accident involved me riding down main street when a guy opened his door on me. I flew so high and landed so hard on my back, it felt like my arms and legs were detaching from my body. Steve jumped off his bike and ran up to the guy and pushed

My Story

him against the car asking him, "What the fuck are you doing? Don't you look in your mirror?"

He was my hero and also a little terrifying. We started making our plans to get married. What a dream come true. I was getting married and I had no idea what that looked like, where we were going, or what our life would be. But I was ready for anything.

Chapter 12

I found a very talented young man to make my wedding dress. We designed it together and it was beautiful. It was a shiny white satin and fitted to my body at the top. The bottom was loose but no flare. It had long sleeves and fake pearls for buttons throughout. I only wore that dress one time after the last fitting to show my mom.

Steve had to leave soon for bootcamp and there was no time to plan a wedding. I didn't want to wear the dress at a ceremony in my house. I actually said to my mom, "This isn't the real wedding, so I will wear my wedding dress later". By this time my mom had a few years of sobriety and had a really great friend named Matt. He gave me away upstairs in our living room.

Everyone stood outside the front door to see us off and my mom yelled, "Oh, we need the rice!" She came running out with a box of Minute Rice and started throwing it at us. We jumped in my black El Camino and attached to the tailgate were three soda cans, hanging from a red shoelace, making a ridiculous sound as we drove off. I loved that moment because that is who we were: simple people and using the resources we had. We never really welcomed the saying that it's all about presentation. Instead, we believed you should hurry up and get it done.

We got stationed in California, which is where I was born, so I was very excited to be there. We found a small apartment about five miles from the beach in Oceanside. We bought a Ford Ranger and I got a job at K-Mart. I tended to make friends pretty easily, and this would be no different. I met a girl named Renee. We became fast friends due to our husbands both being Marines and she was really funny. She was more refined than me and more of a girly girl. Renee had gorgeous blonde hair with natural highlights and big green eyes. She had long eyelashes and a welcoming smile. She was so kind, positive and a great listener.

Renee was from a small town and like me was happy to be in California and married to a Marine. We were able to talk about how hard it was to be a military wife and what it meant to be married. We both believed in God and had our own churches that we continued to attend through our crazy next few years. We both agree the adventures we endured together made us the parents we are today. And without alcohol our choices would have looked much different. Struggles would surely still have occurred but our minds would have been clear.

I got pregnant a couple times in the first two years but had miscarriages both times. Steve asked what was wrong with me that meant I couldn't get pregnant. I told him I could get pregnant;

My Story

I just couldn't make it stay. With each miscarriage a piece of my confidence would be removed and I felt like I was failing, not only as a wife but as a woman. Drinking wasn't a daily thing; it was still just weekends and only when Steve was out of town. But I could feel it was slowly changing my moral compass.

I asked the doctor if this was happening because of alcohol and he said no. He told me this was very common and there was nothing wrong with me. My third try was an ectopic pregnancy. I was having really bad cramps and when I went to the doctor, he was surprised that I had not been in more pain. The egg was stuck in the tubes and was pretty large. After surgery, I knew I was never going to have a baby. So, I decided I was going to live my life to the fullest, work hard, have fun and not worry about having a child.

Chapter 13

Renee and I would find ourselves having a lot of time without our husbands because they would be shipped off for months at a time. From what I recall, the craziness began after a motorcycle ride on the beach. I didn't feel like I was good at flirting but I was very friendly and able to ask for what I wanted. Renee was better at flirting because she had big pretty eyes and a soft voice. We pulled over a couple of boys down by the beach to get a ride on their motorcycles. We didn't have to wear helmets then and honestly it didn't even cross my mind. They asked if we were hungry after the ride, but we declined going for a meal. Renee and I had a thought that we could probably get free meals anytime if we played our cards right.

After a few months at K-Mart I got a job at the PX (post exchange) on base. This was a really bad idea, but it paid more and I would be closer to the beach. The PX was like a free candy store of handsome marines with big smiles who were always ready for fun. Renee and I would get all dressed up for nights on the town. We would go to the clubs on base, then head out off base to continue the evening. Sometimes we would just party at the beach after a long day of volleyball. I was 21 by this stage and had no one telling me what to do or how to do it. It's not that I had that too much before, but now I was legal. The world was a playground, and I wanted to get on all of the rides.

I knew pretty early on that I had made a mistake getting married at such a young age, and Steve being my first real relationship made me even more unsure if I could do this for a long period of time. I thought maybe I could just tell him I changed my mind and we could end it early. He would not concede. Steve was a player in high school and had a lot of experience with the ladies, but he was now ready to settle down. There was a part of me that was curious and wanted to catch up with him and be with more men. I didn't think it was fair that I had been a virgin when we met and he wasn't.

When Steve was home, I played the role of a wife to my understanding. I cooked the chicken and baked the chocolate cake. Any time I would invite him out with my friends he would say, "I don't want to meet your little friends". He didn't want to participate in life outside of me, his job and the gym. I did like going to the gym with him. It felt like old times, but we never talked to anyone, and he really didn't have any friends to go do things with like he did in New Mexico. I think back now and I bet he was pretty lonely at times, being so far from home.

In the military it was said that if the Marine Corps wanted you to have a wife, they would have issued you one. When Steve was overseas six months at a time, Renee and I would hear stories of the guys cheating on their wives. The seeds were constantly being planted, and I watered them with my own imagination of what my husband was or wasn't doing. As I met more boys and built more friendships it was obvious that I was gaining more confidence on what I could control, or at least what looked like control to me. I was getting all the attention a girl could want, and no one was getting hurt.

When guys asked me out, I would let them know I was married, and he was a big guy. The more attention I was getting the more of a game it became. I transformed into this person I didn't know, but I really liked the way I felt. It was like I had God pulling on one hand and the Devil pulling on the other.

I told myself that it was all about balance. I had no idea how strong alcohol was and the slow changes in my brain that were happening. I am in no way blaming alcohol for my actions. I do believe that without it, I would not have made the same choices. It has been said that alcohol actually removes a person's choice. To really understand this, I had to do some real work when I got sober and let go of the control in thinking that I always have a choice.

Chapter 14

Since Steve didn't drink much, I would wait until he left for his six-month tour. I would be so desperate to go out I would ask his officers at the gym when they would be leaving. I would act nonchalant about it, but inside I wanted to grab them by the shoulders and say, "Leave already". I don't know if it was the drink or the attention I was missing more. I continued to think of ways I could get Steve to divorce me by making it his idea.

I knew that bad decisions were coming, but I was so addicted to the attention of other men that I couldn't stop the storm. Steve never made any effort to change, and we didn't have the skills to communicate through any of the issues. How was I going to get out of this situation? I was just too young to be in this marriage and too ignorant to know how to bow out gracefully. So, I stayed and continued to live my life the way I wanted every other six months.

Finally Free

One day, Renee and I were heading to the beach when Steve was coming into town. I didn't wait for him because I knew he would say no, and then I wouldn't be able to go. I left him a note to meet us there for some hotdogs and volleyball. We were with a group of eight or nine people sitting in a circle talking. I saw the person across from me look above my head with big eyes. I felt someone grab the back of my sweatshirt and lift me onto my feet.

Steve decided to come to the beach but he wasn't interested in hotdogs or volleyball. He started yelling at me and stormed off telling me to get home. So, I sat back down, completely embarrassed, and told the group, "Well, that's my husband". We were just not on the same page on anything to do with what a relationship should be, and the inability to communicate just made things more difficult.

We ended up moving in with Renee and her husband so we could all save money. We first moved into a small house that Renee rented. Soon after we found a bigger apartment in a pretty small complex. One night we were all home watching a movie. Renee came and sat next to me. She looked up and whispered, "Jeff and Chris were in a motorcycle accident, Chris is in a coma and Jeff didn't make it".

Jeff was a guy that I had been hanging out with for a couple months. He was also a Marine and we spent most of our time at the beach or his house listening to music and drinking. We were always in a big group. I had wanted to leave Steve so I could be with Jeff but I really thought Steve might hurt Jeff so it wasn't an option.

I quickly jumped up and ran into my room. Renee followed and gave me more information about the accident. Jeff and Chris were only two houses down from making it home. It was dark and a large semi-truck was parked on the wrong side of the street without its parking lights on or cones. Jeff and Chris had been drinking and hit the truck so hard Jeff flew underneath the car by his house.

Renee and I rushed to the scene. I remember the smell of blood and water as they were washing down the street. I saw the blood spattered across the semi, and Chris was in the ambulance leaving the scene. I saw them pull Jeff's body out from under the car and his head was the size of a small melon. It is incredible how much your eyes can see in a quick moment. I picked up a couple pieces of his motorcycle and his flesh on them. I was crying so hard, and Renee was consoling me. I had never felt that uncontrollable emotion thus far in my life. I had no idea what would happen when I got home, but I would take it on the chin, however it came.

Chapter 15

Generally, when there was a fight or flight situation in my life I would choose to fight, not with fists but with words. We headed up the stairs to the apartment and Renee and I were trying to prepare ourselves. I walked straight to my room, tears falling down my face. I just couldn't stop crying. Steve was already in the room with a gun pointed at me as I walked in. He pointed it at me and said, "I should shoot you, then you can be with him."

I told him that Jeff and I were just friends and to go ahead and do it. The doorbell rang and I wiped my tears and answered the door. I knew God was trying to help us but I can be so hard-headed. Two missionaries were at the door. I whispered to them not to leave. Right then Steve came around the corner in their view and he didn't have a shirt on so his muscles were everywhere. If smoke could actually come out of our heads when we get angry, you would have seen it coming out of his.

Finally Free

The boys looked at him and took off down the stairs so fast their ties were flying behind them. God sent them to get things calmed down, which it did. Again, I asked for a divorce and again was denied. I just couldn't understand why he wouldn't leave me. I was obviously not a good wife or the person he wanted to be with. Or was I, and I just needed some guidance? After this incident I just became quiet for a few weeks. I was really trying to figure out how to be in this marriage and still drink and have fun.

Steve and I later moved into a house with some family members who wanted to share the rent. Things just never got better and we both knew it. I found a place that did divorces for 90 bucks. I printed out the paperwork and gave it to Steve to sign. I offered to be the one to move out since it was my idea. I could see the hurt in his face as he grabbed the papers and said, "Who the fuck do you think you are?" I had no idea who I was. I just apologized and walked away. I swore I would never be in this situation again where I would hurt someone. I was able to apologize again to Steve years later and he jokingly told me, "Just so you know I was really sick of chicken and chocolate cake."

Chapter 16

After Steve moved out, I dated so much that the song, "Another one bites the dust" was a running joke in the house when my date would pick me up. It didn't take long for me to meet someone I really fell for. I had a hard time sticking to my declarations. They felt real and effective in the moment and quickly deteriorated when a new shiny toy came around. I was free and loving life. I was ready for what came next, and I would have fun no matter what. That was my theme to every situation. I didn't like being sad or depressed. I just wasn't good at it, and I didn't like people feeling sorry for me.

Mike was tall, blonde, tan and hot as hell. He had a killer smile and loved hanging at the beach. We liked the same music, and he was never jealous, as far as I knew. Renee also got a divorce, so we were now hanging out with Mike and his friend Carl. Carl had dark hair and big puppy dog eyes. He was tan and just as hot as Mike. It was like walking around with two Ken dolls. Work, beach, volleyball, party, shower, party: that would be my routine for the next few years.

Finally Free

I was really happy with my life and I wanted Mike to move in with me. We even took a Spanish class together at the local college. He passed, I didn't. He studied; I didn't. I just liked being with him. I didn't care if I learned Spanish. But the teacher did tell me I was very close and could come back without charge. I told her if I was that close then she should just pass me. Mike and I settled into this relationship and things were really good.

Then I got pregnant. Mike decided we should take a trip to meet his family. We drove out to Fresno and I met his mom and sisters. They were very young considering he was in his 20s. We went to some waterfalls close by and slid down some rocks. I hit my tailbone so hard on a rock it left a huge black bruise on my butt. It was a blast.

While we were at the top, I heard someone yell my name. It was someone from Oceanside. To this day I can't remember who it was. Mike didn't seem put off about this, but he did make a comment about how I know people wherever I go. After the waterfalls, we went to the beach. We were laying out talking about our "situation."

Mike asked if I would consider getting an abortion and I quickly said "No way". We talked a little more and then he went for a swim. His mom laid down beside me to share her thoughts. She told me that Mike had his whole life ahead of him and that he was not ready for a baby. I remember thinking, "You're old and you have these little kids, why are you saying this?" I just listened and wished I would have driven myself so I could leave right then.

Chapter 17

Later that evening we went to the local bar. I knew that I wasn't going to drink, because I had literally just found out I was pregnant. Mike had invited an old girlfriend to the bar. At first, I didn't even take in what was happening and was super happy to meet her. He was trying to make me jealous and uncomfortable. It got to the point that they were hugging and flirting with each other so I left and walked back to the house.

It was a few miles away and I really had no idea where I was. I just kept thinking about the baby and what a great mom I would be. Then thoughts of the miscarriages came in and I thought, I will probably miscarry so it doesn't matter. It was only a couple weeks so I had time to figure it out. I prayed so hard but back then I didn't really hang around for the answers from God. It was basically like the game telephone. I put the prayer out there, then it would go through all the little monkeys in my brain, then the final distorted answer would come back to me and I'd act.

Finally Free

The ride home was very long and quiet. So many uncertainties. I thought of my life; of not having a dad and how my brothers and I all had different donors. The things we missed out on; how could I do that to a baby? I told myself it wouldn't be impossible. I named it Stevie Lynn before even knowing it was a boy or girl. There was no way I was going to get an abortion.

I was in California and my mom and grandma were in New Mexico. I couldn't talk to them about it, I had to make this decision on my own. Maybe tomorrow I would have a miscarriage and I wouldn't have to choose. All of these thoughts were going a hundred miles an hour in my sober brain. What would I do, how could I live with myself either way? I knew that I could overcome whatever decision I make no matter what. It would be best to sleep on it and we could talk more in the morning.

Instead, Mike told me he had herpes. I had no idea what that meant when he said it. I knew I didn't, so was it possible that he had been with someone else? How dare he cheat on me, the cheater herself. Was this payback for my behavior through my marriage? I thought it must have been. I was being punished. He then said he got it from someone who he had been seeing. I lost it. I started to punch the closet door and quickly realized I didn't want to hurt my right hand on the wall and the closet was that thin cardboard. So, I put my left hand through the closet door.

I immediately felt like an idiot. I was completely defeated the next day as I was watching Montel. It was about adult children who were trying to find their biological father. The hurt and pain they were expressing just hit me so hard. I told Mike that he would need to

My Story

take me to the doctor. I didn't talk to him the whole way there or the whole way back.

I prayed for forgiveness before and after and every day after that. There was no one to counsel me or talk me out of this. I literally called, made the appointment while crying, walked in, and that was it. I called my mom after. She told me about her experience that I shared in the first part of this book. That was even more heartbreaking. Maybe if I had known her story sooner, just maybe, my decision would have been different.

Chapter 18

There is much controversy in the world today about this topic. I generally stay very neutral when it is brought up in conversation. Now, I can share my true thoughts on this matter. If you have not been in the situation there is no possible way you can feel what the person is going through. No one is excited to make this choice. No one forgets the choice was made. No one can change or wash away this memory. What the person can do is talk about it to others who have been there and find a way to move through it.

I knew this part of my book was going to be difficult but I will do no justice for anyone if I leave it out. So much more goes into it than a quote, "It's my body, It's my choice". I do think about the what ifs. What if I had these people at the front door of the facility I went to, trying to convince me to make another choice. It is moot at this point. I understand both sides and I have compassion for both sides. This may still sound neutral to some but others who

Finally Free

have had this experience will know what my heart and mind are sharing with you.

I knew I had to get back into life and the best place for me to be was church. I started hanging out with more people from church and going to singles activities. It was still uncomfortable because I just didn't fit. I felt like they knew but they would never judge me for it. I connected with an old friend from school who was now living in Utah. I only planned to go for a week. I loved it there so much that I got a job on 8th and 8th at a Smith's grocery store and stayed over a month. I was really considering just living there.

This friend was the same friend growing up who gave me a ride to church. She was married at this point but was cool enough to go to a dance with me. Outside the dance I was taking a break to cool off and a couple guys came up and asked if I wanted a drink. I couldn't believe it. Do I have "I love alcohol" written on my forehead? Luckily my friend has a nose like a hound dog and I wasn't about to get a tongue lashing from her. So, I just gave them my number and told them we would meet up another day.

I like to keep my promises so I met up with one of them when my friend was busy with work. We headed up some popular hill where people make out and other things, I am sure. It was kind of weird being with a Mormon boy. I pretty much stayed away from them because I didn't want them to change me and I certainly didn't want to change them to be like me. The guy convinced me that he really liked me and for some reason it just felt special.

My Story

We ended up having sex and he started crying right after. I don't know if this was some kind of game these boys play or what was happening. It was the first "out of body" experience I had ever had. I couldn't get out of there fast enough. In my mind, because we were both Mormons and he initiated, it was okay. I swear as I am typing this, I am realizing just how lost I was.

Would I ever get it together and be normal? Is this normal? What is wrong with me? Am I bringing these experiences into my life just by existing? Will I ever feel special enough to be important to another human? Is it because I didn't know my father or because I was molested? Is it the alcohol or the way I look? Should I join another church that allows you to do what you want and doesn't have any rules to make you feel guilty? Yes, all of these thoughts were floating around and around my mind. I had to get the hell out of Utah.

Chapter 19

Awe yes, back in California. Okay, time for a fresh start. Stay away from men, work out, get a job, find positive friends. I found a job as a nanny for a couple of anesthesiologists. Very nice couple. They had two boys and a girl. I had never been a nanny before so I wasn't sure what it would entail. It was a live-in position so I didn't have to pay rent, which is a great thing when you're single and living in Rancho Santa Fe.

All I had was a dresser from my friend Jeff who passed away, a surfboard, some clothes and my El Camino. The wife was kind of eccentric. She would call me from the driveway to let me know she was in the driveway. Back then they had those really big car phones. The husband was really active with the kids and very nice. He would invite me to bike ride with all of them when I was off work because his wife didn't want to go. She really liked to read magazines.

They had a little one just learning to walk. I got him to walk one day and I wanted to show the mom his progress. When she got home,

Finally Free

I asked her to help him walk because I thought he was close. She was hesitant but finally helped him walk. Not much excitement though. I guess I had higher expectations. The mom would call me in the morning, using the house speakers, to have me come and get him off of her lap. This was super sad. But I was happy I got to spend time with him.

The older boy liked playing every sport so we were very active in the back yard and at the local pool. The little girl just wanted to be herself. She told me she hated the way her clothes were folded in her drawers so I helped her reorganize all of them. She was so excited and when her mom came home, she ran to show her. Her mom immediately started folding everything back to the way it was. I don't recall the mom ever hugging any of them but the dad made up for that.

This job was tough because I never knew what the wife was going to have me do day to day. There was no routine. One day it was the kids, another day it was cleaning. She actually wanted me to clean a room that had nothing in it. I never did. One thing I really liked was when they went out of town. I was allowed to have friends over. I only had my family and one guy friend over.

I met this chef, well actually he was a surfer who could cook really well. I brought him to the mansion and he made the best dinner for us. He asked if he could shower because we had been at the beach. We weren't dating or anything which made it easy to be around him. I was in the kitchen cleaning up and I remembered how slippery the tubs could be. I ran back to tell him, then all of a sudden, I heard a loud bang. We were laughing so hard and he was

My Story

trying to get up and his long curly black hair was getting caught under his hands. We played house for a while then he left. I was in this huge house, by myself, so of course, I got to go to the bars on the beach because I can't sit still.

Chapter 20

I settled into the realization that I was raising someone else's kids while the parents were making a shit ton of money. I built relationships with the other workers on the property and some of the neighbors. I had been wanting a tattoo for quite some time and was making pretty good money so I could afford it. I was thinking about getting the Maui Shark holding a surfboard on my ankle. My friend Blake, who was a businessman, said not to get something so big in case I got a job and I had to wear pantyhose and high heels.

I told Blake I would never want a professional job where I would have to wear pantyhose and high heels. But I agreed that the Maui Shark may be a little too much. I liked the "BAD BOY" symbol but wanted something more feminine. I met with the artist and he said he would draw up a "BAD GIRL" cartoon character and give me a call when it was ready. Living in a military town everyone had tattoos so it wasn't a big deal and I had waited long enough.

Finally Free

The tattoo guy called but I was watching the baby during the time he was wanting me to come to the shop. It was the baby's nap time so he could fall asleep in the car and I could just take the car seat in with me. This worked like a charm. He stayed asleep the whole time and in case he woke up I had him facing some cartoon characters on the wall. This is just one more example of the selfishness and self-seeking which was a huge part of my life and I was in complete denial it even existed. I just called anything crazy that I did an "experience".

 At dinner the wife asked if I hurt my leg. I told her I got a tattoo. I was rarely interested in lying. I was told if you lie you have to keep lying and that just seemed like a lot of work. Now, not saying anything, that I find more appealing. She didn't ask when I did it and that was that. Things were going okay with the job but I was very bored and I didn't like the lack of interest the mom had for the kids. I started contemplating my escape plan. I really had a good bond with the kids but I thought if I left maybe the mom would have to pay attention to them. After all, she only worked a couple days a week. This was me justifying my escape early on and having no good reason for jumping ship.

The wife was going to have a get together and wanted the whole house cleaned meticulously; which is pretty much what it was every day. I assumed I would be watching the kids while she brought in help for cleaning. This was not the case at all. She informed me she had her old nanny coming to watch the kids while I clean. She brought me over to the stove and showed me how she wanted it cleaned underneath the top cover. As she was talking, I was getting Cinderella syndrome running through my head.

My Story

I told myself, "You're better than this," and when she left the house, I quickly found the phone book and started looking for a job. I called a child care facility called "Our Gang". The owner answered and asked if I could come in for an interview in a couple hours. I agreed and ran outside and grabbed a couple of the Mexican workers and had them help me load up my black dresser, clothes and I was out of there. I let the old nanny know I was leaving. She didn't say a word. I left so fast I forgot my surfboard. I could be very reactive, but I thought I was just really flexible and a take charge kind of person.

Chapter 21

I drove up to the facility wearing cut-off jean shorts, tank top and flip flops. I went into the office and this classy woman dressed in a professional outfit, pantyhose and all greeted me. I gave a little history of my work experience and she said, "When can you start?" I literally dropped to my knees and thanked her. I ran out to my El Camino and as I tried to open my door, I spotted my keys in the car and the door was locked. When the locksmith showed up, I gave him my sob story and he opened my door for free.

As I was driving away, I realized I didn't have anywhere to live. I got the newspaper and found a room for rent. I drove to the house and they let me move in. There was another girl renting one of the other rooms upstairs next to mine. The couple that brought us in were the same religion as me, so I was sure this would be a chill place to stay. We became fast friends. Things were going well for a short time. The husband from my old nanny job brought my surfboard to my new daycare job. I actually hid in the closet because I felt so guilty for not saying goodbye to him or the kids.

One day, the other roommate and I were upstairs in the bathroom trying to figure out what was happening downstairs. The wife was yelling at her husband and he was just trying to calm her down. She was running around with a knife accusing him of cheating on her. Me and the other roommate were trying to figure out an exit plan. We both decided to leave for good so we got all of our things packed up. When I grabbed the surfboard, I saw that the wife had cut the cord off of it. We helped each other load up our cars and off we went.

As I was driving away, into the night, the dresser flew out of my El Camino with all of my clothes and hit a small truck behind me. I pulled over and the guy was super nice and no damage was done to his truck. He helped me get my clothes off the road and the dresser was flattened so nothing could be done about that. I was driving around trying to figure out what to do and where to go from here. Some of the girls from my new job had a house and let me stay there until I figured it out.

My life became a "Friends" episode. Just a group of friends living life, work, party, relationships, etc. Life couldn't be any better. But there was something missing. I was meeting a lot of great guys but nothing stuck. I would always find something wrong with them and pull myself out of the relationship if it got too close. I wanted a baby. I was nearing the age of 27 and I knew I would be a great mom but I wasn't finding dad and husband material. I didn't really want a husband but I really wanted a baby.

Chapter 22

We all went to a club in Oceanside called In Cahoots to go dancing and I met a guy named Greg. He was older and he was a cowboy. He wore a black hat and looked like George Strait, the country singer. He had the whitest teeth and a crooked smile. He was a gentleman and that was a weird feeling. I felt like I was more mature around him. We dated for a while but decided we were better friends. We decided to move in together to save money. That was definitely a thing in California.

I didn't want to live where Greg lived so I told him I would find an apartment in La Jolla. I found a super nice two bedroom near the temple. It was only $750 a month back then. Greg liked to read the paper and drink coffee. I just wasn't quite ready for that lifestyle but I did see how peaceful he looked when he was on the patio at the little table. It reminded me of the times I see people sitting on their porch just looking out into the road. I liked the way it looked but I didn't want to do it. He knew he never wanted kids and he decided to get vasectomy. I tried to talk him out of it because he might find a young girl who wanted to have kids and he only had one son. He told me he could just get it reversed if that was the case.

Greg's son was a movie star at the time and a very sweet kid. We took him to an Eagles concert and he would come over and swim. After we dropped him off at home one night, I got the back story on Greg and his wife's relationship. There are always many sides to stories so I just listened and changed the conversation. I had no experience to share in this situation that would be helpful.

Greg and I continued to go out dancing at In Cahoots. We saw Billy Ray Cyrus there back when he wore his overalls and no shirt. Greg may have been a missed opportunity to have a child with but I just couldn't wrap my head around how settled he was. Of course, now I can see how amazing that could have been had I been willing.

One day my work friends and I were hanging out at the house by the beach. I was kind of quiet which is a red flag to my friends that something is going on. They asked me what was wrong. I told them I wanted to be a mom and I just couldn't find the right guy. They grabbed me and said, "We're going out". We walked into In Cahoots, and the search began. It's interesting thinking about what you want in a donor. The only thing I had immediate access to is how he would look. It takes a while to actually get to know someone and I just didn't have the time or the desire.

For this adventure I would need to find someone who would be willing to have a baby with no strings attached or I would have to fall in love. The first scenario sounded easier. As I was walking down the aisle, I saw this guy in a peach V-neck shirt. My first thought was, "Huh I didn't think men wore the color peach, he's probably gay". I quickly moved my eyes up to his face. He had gigantic blue eyes and a great smile. He wasn't very tall and not as muscular as the guys I was usually attracted to. I asked him where he was going and he said, "To dance with you". It was on.

Chapter 23

Those four little words would be the beginning of the coolest adventure of my life. I will call him Chester for the purpose of this part of my story. Our dates consisted of motorcycle rides, beach time, and not much partying which was really cool. He liked to come hang out at my apartment because he didn't have his own place. One time we went to the beach and he serenaded me with the song, "Feed Jake". He definitely had talent but was he the one to father my baby?

The more I got to know him, more red flags started to appear. If I was going to do this, I needed to have the conversation with him. I had told him the first night we met that I wanted to have a baby with no strings attached. He said, "I could make that happen, I already have two kids by two different moms". Any normal girl would run for the hills but to me this sounded perfect. He also said he would cover the medical since he was in the Navy. After the conversation we continued hanging out as regularly as two single people could hang out.

Finally Free

Chester met us girls at the house down by the beach. He showed up with a black eye and the same peach shirt. What was it with this shirt? When we asked what happened he said he got into a fight with some Navy guys. Like any normal girl, I found that super attractive. The house had hardwood floors so I thought I would show off by skating out the door and I ran into the point of a palm tree. My hand immediately went numb and was cut into a very thin V shape. Chester took me to the emergency room. The doctor said he wanted to do a blood test to check for poison. I said to Chester, "Wouldn't it be funny if it came back that I was pregnant". He said, "This would be a great 'remember when'".

Not long after that day I had to go back to the doctor. I was having a difficult time breathing and I did have a history of asthma. Dr. Diamont was very friendly and asked me to do a urine test as well as a blood test. I asked him if he was checking if I was pregnant and he said no but he could if I wanted him to. After the appointment I went home and waited for the results.

Greg and I were watching a movie and eating my famous top ramen, with melted cheddar cheese and chili. I also make this with tuna sometimes. For some reason I thought it was healthy as long as I poured out the little packet that came inside the package. The phone rang and it was the doctor. It was pretty late so I was surprised to hear his voice. What he would say would change my life forever.

"Carol," he said. "You are pregnant." We didn't have a speaker phone then but my roommate Greg could tell by my face that something big had happened. I calmly said thank you and hung up the phone. "Oh my gosh, oh my gosh, I am going to have a baby," I yelled. I

My Story

just started crying because I couldn't believe it had happened. It really worked and I was going to get my very own baby and I could do whatever I wanted and raise it however I wanted because I was single. For this same reason my tears changed to fear and I asked Greg, "Holy shit what am I going to do?" Greg actually offered to marry me right away. It was the sweetest thing ever, but I didn't work this hard to just marry someone. No, I wanted to go through whatever was coming next on my own. No other thoughts came to my mind other than "I am going to be the best mom in the world".

Chapter 24

My immediate family was still in New Mexico at this time. I was talking with my Cali friends trying to figure out a way to stay in California. My brother kept saying it would be better if I moved back so we could raise our kids together and have barbecues. I definitely wanted my baby to be around my grandma and my mom and could use their help babysitting while I was working. My ex-husband and his family were there as well and we had remained friends through all of that negativity. I had two good options and out of courtesy I thought I should run it by Chester in case he wanted to be close to the baby geographically.

As I sat at work looking at all the kids I had bonded with and their parents it was really a difficult decision. Chester was out of town and I wanted to wait and talk to him face to face. That thought lasted about a second. It took a few times of me calling and leaving messages for him to respond. I told Chester what my thoughts were and he quickly said, "Let's talk about this when I get back to

Finally Free

California". I could tell by his tone it was not going to be a difficult decision to move back to New Mexico.

Chester arrived at my apartment soon after his return to California from Texas. He asked if he could take a bath. This is another thing I didn't know men did. Anyway, I was sitting on the floor next to the tub and we were talking about how cool this was and I couldn't believe it actually worked. He then asked me, "Would you consider getting an abortion?" I know my face answered that question, but just in case I said disappointingly, "No, that is not an option".

This was super painful considering we had the whole thing lined out and were in agreement that he had no commitment to the baby. I then asked why he would even ask me that when this was the sole purpose of us even hanging out. Imagine two selfish people having this conversation. It looks even more ridiculous as I am writing it out. Bath time ended and he said he was only asking because he has two kids with two different moms already. And I responded, "Yes, and you don't take care of them either so what is the problem?" Later I would find out he had much more baggage to unpack and I was grateful that I would be in New Mexico before it was revealed.

Well, back to New Mexico we went. No plan, just another experience and adventure were put into play. I said goodbye to my friends, co-workers, boss, and all the little children that filled up my life working at "Our Gang". It was also very difficult to leave my roommate and friend Greg. We made a deal that he would be my baby's Godfather and my friend Renee would be the Godmother. Greg and I also said if neither of us married by the time we were 60 we would marry each other. When I say goodbye to people, I truly believe we will see each other again. It rarely works out that way in the real world.

Goodbye, for now, California and hello to the most incredible future. I loved starting over. I was good at it. I lived simply so there was little stress in moving and I was going back to a place I grew up from the age of nine. I was going to be back with my family, get a great job, and raise my little baby in a town I didn't want to live in but I was determined to make this work. This probably sounds familiar. I was already trying to figure out how to get back to California before I ever left it.

I wondered, would I ever settle into a place and never want to leave? If there was an emptiness inside me would this little creature fill it up? Was God really trusting me with one of his babies? Would I change, and if so, who would I become?

Chapter 25

Because my mom lived in the same house I grew up in, I didn't need to find a place to live right away. It was a four bedroom and it was only her and my youngest brother. I quickly connected with some friends from high school and visited my grandma and Jack. My grandma met Jack on an airplane when she was in her early 70s. When she talked about him, she fought back how happy she really was. We told her it was okay to be happy. My grandma wasn't big on sharing her emotions but she couldn't help it when it came to Jack. She called him the Jack of all trades. He really could do anything and was a very kind man.

I remember going to a dance hall with them, I believe it was called the "Elks Club". I had never seen my grandma drink alcohol so it was weird when the waitress set down a cocktail. I asked, "Oh so you drink alcohol now?" She just smiled and said she just ordered it to sip. And she literally took one sip the whole night. Living with an alcoholic of my grandpa's sort could make one very cautious. Good thing she didn't know how I drank.

Finally Free

Jack grabbed my hand and off to the dance floor we went. He told me that I was as stiff as a broomstick. I wanted to tell him it was super creepy dancing with my grandma's husband but I just laughed. I used humor throughout my life when things got weird or uncomfortable. I really liked making people laugh and sometimes, unknowingly, at the expense of others. I learned later it was sarcasm and it can be very hurtful. Life lessons started coming to light more frequently as I was getting older and more self-aware.

Overall, I was happy to be in a familiar place and everyone was very excited about the baby. My grandma brought up college of course and I figured I was probably going to need to get a career type job now that I was going to be a mom. I decided I was going to look into being a PE teacher as soon as the baby was older. Soon we were picking out baby furniture, clothes, snot squeezing things, bottles, and tiny Michael Jordan shoes for when the baby was walking.

I wasn't going to be wearing maternity clothes so I got a couple pairs of overalls that my belly could grow into. I never thought about gaining weight or morning sickness. I just thought about how cute my baby was going to be and how much fun we were going to have together. I took my brother's old room and this brought back so many good memories. We used to sit in our closets when we got sent to our rooms and talk through the walls.

We played "Chinese restaurant". This consisted of us speaking in Chinese and acting like I was the waitress and my brother was the customer. He would make me mad and I would kick him out of the restaurant then we both started laughing. Sometimes we would record it then play it back so we could fix any mistakes on the next take. When we played it for my mom she would just laugh and tell us we were very creative. I have no idea where this came from because I never even ate Chinese food until I was in my 20s.

It was time to paint the baby's room. I didn't know if I was having a girl or a boy but I wasn't going to paint it pink because that was expected and not original. I painted it dark blue with a white picket fence and white clouds. My mom used to tell us we would live in a house one day with a white picket fence and I wanted the same for my own baby. And there it was.

After I finished painting, I stood back and said out loud, "Honey doesn't that look great!" And as a joke, I responded, "Oh yes, there is no honey". This was a proud and sad moment. Then my mom came in and some friends came over and loved it and the self-pity quickly went away. I ended up finding a cute border to go along on top of the fence and the room was complete. Now I just needed to figure out what I was going to do for the next nine months.

Chapter 26

I had already known I wasn't going to drink alcohol while I was pregnant but I could still go to the bars and dance because I wasn't showing. My friends and I went to the "Top Deck", which was a local dance club. It was so fun because I had so many classmates who still lived in town. I didn't feel any different being pregnant early on. When guys asked me if they could buy me a beer, I would jokingly say, "I'm pregnant but you can give me the money you were going to spend". We would laugh and go dance.

It didn't seem to bother men and it felt like I had this super power. I went to dinner with some friends and I remember someone had bought me a Coors Light. Not even thinking about it, I put it up to my lips, stopped and was like, oh my gosh I almost drank that. It's interesting that I had no problem putting this poison in my own body but it was not going to be in my baby's body. This made me hyper-focused on putting myself in these situations and going to the club was not a good place for me to be.

Finally Free

I joined a bowling league and was still surrounded by alcohol. Where on earth could I go have fun and not be tempted to drink alcohol? I needed to find some non-drinking friends. I remembered the 12-step program my mom attended and figured that would be a good place to start. I went to the meeting and actually felt right at home. I knew my mom's friends and it was not a tough group to join. I started attending at least a meeting a day. I didn't have anyone ask me if they could mentor me or work through any steps, and I certainly wasn't going to ask them. I just went and talked to people, listened to their experiences and shared what I was going through being pregnant and not drinking.

There were always activities at parks with my new non-drinking friends and plenty of opportunities to practice my counseling skills. I didn't start showing until much later in my pregnancy and when someone would ask me out, I would get a little annoyed. My focus was shifting and I was thinking less of my wants and needs and more about the baby. I didn't want to share my baby with just any guy. The whole plan was to raise this baby the way I wanted with no one telling me how to do it. Especially a man.

When I got my first ultrasound, they told me it looked like I was having a girl. I told them they needed to look again because I was having a boy. I didn't want a girl because I didn't want her to go through all of the hard things girls have to go through. Like buying tampons. My experience with my period was so awkward. I was on the toilet and yelled to Mom, "Mom, come here!" And through the door I yelled, "Go get those things from the store please". I couldn't even say the word, much less go into a store and buy them. That little video in 6th grade isn't really that helpful. This is my shout out to young girls and parents, guardians whoever is raising them. Talk to them about everything. It truly makes a difference.

Chapter 27

Second ultrasound. "Yes, it's a girl", the ultrasound lady says in a happy voice. I asked if she could do just one more because I was sure I was supposed to have a boy. I already had a name for a boy, Catlin O'Brian. Me and my friend Renee even called guys in the phone book with this last name during our crazy days to see if we could find a single guy so I could marry him and I would have that last name. Talk about trying to control things. I was having a girl. I had this crazy past life and I now had to change everything, figure out how to protect her and still let her be who she is. This shouldn't be difficult at all.

I went into labor and I was on the phone with a high school friend while lying in the hospital bed. She was talking and all of a sudden, the sound of everything just faded away. I remember this excruciating pain and quietly said, "I got to go" and dropped the phone. This is what I remember. There were a lot of people in my room, they were giving me something in my arm because I was only two centimeters. The baby's heart rate changed and they said the baby didn't like the medicine. The doctor came in and said, "We are going to do a C-Section".

I remembered this from class but I really didn't care until they were wheeling me off into surgery. I just remember seeing pink elephants and laughing saying out loud that I just peed and I don't have to clean it up. I also said my vagina will be the same size because they are taking the baby out of my stomach. People in the room were laughing and telling me everything was okay. As we were getting on the elevator I was crying and I said, "I can't even have a baby the right way". Imagine being in the space of excitement and this negative thought comes and tries to diminish this beautiful moment. Plus, they gave me drugs so that's how present I really was.

My mom was in the surgical room with me. She sat where she could hold my hand, see my face, then on the other side of the curtain, she could see baby Dakota being born. They lifted Dakota above the sheet, she did one cry, "Ma", then they took her off to clean her up. I said, "That's nice", then fell asleep. Her name was chosen at my baby shower. I had said I wanted a name that is strong like a state and people can't make fun of too much. A lady at the bowling alley told me that Dakota was an Indian Tribe name which was really cool.

Later that day it was time for me to feed her and the nurse who came in had the bedside manner of an angry bull. I was gently trying to figure out how to do this breast-feeding thing and she just grabbed my boob and shoved it in the baby's mouth. I thanked her of course as she quickly exited the room. I thought about how fun the classes were preparing for this beautiful baby and how much I totally forgot when it actually came time to use the skills taught. My mom did the classes with me and sometimes my grandma. Those were great moments and also sad because everyone else had a husband or boyfriend.

On day two I had finished a much-needed shower and I went down the hall to get my baby. In the 90s they kept the babies together in another room so the moms could rest. I found Dakota and started wheeling her to my room. The nurse stopped me and asked, "What are you doing?" I let her know that I was taking my baby to my room to feed her. She said, "That's not your baby". I started laughing but I really felt like an idiot for not recognizing my own baby. The nurse said the babies get moved around the room so they won't be in the same spot. She told me I had to look at the name tag. Holy crap, this was already too hard, how would I keep this baby safe when I almost traded her for a boy named Miguel?

I was so excited to show Dakota her room. But first I would stay at my grandma's so she could help me heal and take care of Dakota. On the second day home I was putting on my blue jeans and as I zipped them up, I caught the zipper on my incision and a gush of blood started pouring out. I screamed for my grandma and she called the doctor. It was just a hematoma. I learned more about the human body through this experience than I ever did in school. I calmed down quickly, as if I knew what that was and got myself cleaned up.

I loved spending every moment with Dakota. Before she was even born, she was my world and I was going to do everything I could

Finally Free

to make sure she had a great life. One evening when she was a few weeks old I was holding her. I was in a chair made of wood with a cowboy print on the cushion. I was looking into her eyes with such awe. And then she looked back into mine. At that moment I knew that she knew I was her mom. She could see into my soul and I could see into hers.

Chapter 28

Dakota started learning new things and of course she was the cutest and smartest baby in the world. She walked before she was one and potty trained before she was two. I didn't have access to anything online so I was just winging it most of the time with the support of her great grandma. We all read to her often and my mom was great at giving her baths in the kitchen sink. I preferred the tub so I could teach her to swim and hold her breath. By three she could do this in a swimming pool.

One day at the pool another little girl around six years old wanted to play with her on the steps. I was in one of the chairs close by watching them. Dakota was able to play on her own and had done so, many times before. In a split second, Dakota's hand slipped off the bar and out of the hands of the little girl. I immediately jumped up and started running toward her as she went under. I remember seeing a man on the other end of the pool. I heard this voice say stop running and jumped.

Finally Free

I jumped into the pool and swooped Dakota up out of the water. I quickly took her to the chair and started comforting her as she was spitting out water. She looked up at me and asked, "Who's the man with the big hands?" I looked over and that man was still at the other end of the pool. I just started crying and I knew then that Jesus was going to take care of this little girl and she would never be too far away from him.

On Dakota's third birthday I got her a bike with training wheels. We had many friends over and a lot of kids. When I brought the bike in, another little boy jumped on it and grabbed it away from her. She let go without hesitation. It took some convincing that it was her bike then we headed outside to give it a whirl. She was getting really good on it but one day she wasn't looking and ran into the back of a parked car.

She got off the bike and wouldn't get back on. I said, "If you're not going to ride it maybe we should give it to the neighbor". She looked at me, paused, and said, "Yes, let's give it to my friend". So much for manipulating this little genius. Eventually she got back on but I had to change my tactic of reverse psychology.

She was very independent, as many single parent children are. I started college and was going to get a teaching degree. Dakota went to the daycare on campus. I could hardly focus on school because I just wanted to hang out with her. And I just really didn't like school. I had a few high school friends in my classes which made it more fun. I had to do all extra credit activities to pass the math classes. Once I gave blood. That was the easiest extra credit I ever earned. It also made me become a regular blood donor.

My Story

Dakota was such a fun, respectful, funny kid. She rarely asked for anything and didn't even ask for things at the checkout stand when grocery shopping. I had a little snack drawer made for her at home so she could access snacks as needed. She still asked me any time she wanted a snack. I taught her how to make her breakfast so I could sleep just a little longer in the morning. I would pour just enough milk into her cup and put it in the fridge for her cereal.

It was so cute watching her choose her cereal, get her bowl and spoon and pour her milk. Like most moms I'm sure, we just can't sleep when they are awake. She was so tiny and so smart. When she was seven, she was able to make eggs and pancakes. When she was eight, she made me eggs for Mother's Day. I bring these things up because I wonder, if I was married would I have encouraged such independence and would I have valued these precious moments?

In church they had something called family home evening. This is where families sing songs, have an activity, read scriptures and have a treat. Since it was just the two of us, I had to be creative. I was never traditional in anything else so why would this be any different? We skipped the songs and went right to an activity or took a trip somewhere like the park or the beach. I figured as long as we were together it was family time and that's what God wanted. It was tough being a single mom, alcoholic and a member of a church that has many guidelines that can be construed as rules. I never felt like I was three different people, just very busy. I had to make this work so Dakota would feel safe and know that she is loved and protected.

Chapter 29

Because I had so much help from the grandmas it was easy to start being social again and hanging out with friends in the evening. I started hiking more and loved taking Dakota with me everywhere I went, except the bars of course. Drinking socially was picking up again and for some reason the loneliness started creeping in. I started looking at myself differently.

I was unconsciously seeking a father for my awesome daughter from time to time. I didn't learn much from my previous wifey experience and I wasn't really that interested in becoming one again. But there was part of me that was feeling bad that Dakota didn't have a dad. When I was taking her to school one day I was at the light and there was a lot of traffic. I asked the crossing guard, "Why is there so much traffic?" She let us know it was Father's Day. Dakota looked over at me with this sad face I had not seen before. I quickly said, "Well I guess you don't have to go to school today," and we headed to the lake.

Finally Free

This would happen every year in church as well. It was tough listening to all the great father-child relationships knowing that I could not make that happen for either of us. I still knew that as long as Dakota knew I loved her and I taught her that anything was possible she would have a different and better life than I gave myself. As she got older it was up to her if we attended events on Father's Day or did something else. We generally did something else.

I tried dating again but it just never went the way I wanted. Then I reconnected with my old babysitter, Michelle. This was the boost into fun I needed. She was now a single mom and we both loved country music, dancing, karaoke and our girls. Her two daughters were a little older and they took Dakota under their little wings. We took the girls to karaoke at a local restaurant and the girls made up a dance to the song, "Genie in a Bottle".

Both of us also liked to drink and talk about everything. We talked often about how we should stop drinking and tried a few times. This was usually the day after a long night of drinking when all we wanted to do was drink water and eat mashed potato tacos. We were perfect friends. We signed off on each other's bullshit and any problems we had were always someone else's fault. We encouraged each other through hard times and celebrated all the good ones.

I was mastering the parent role and felt I was becoming a little too normal. I was having to schedule my drinking around my life. By this time, I was sure I was an alcoholic, especially after going to all those meetings while I was pregnant. A head full of recovery and a belly full of alcohol doesn't mix well. This is where controlled drinking was very effective. If there was something I had to take

My Story

care of the next day early in the morning, I would drink earlier in the evening the night before or not at all. If Dakota was staying over at her grandma's, I would stay out as late as possible and drink as much as I could because I didn't know when I was going to be able to go out again.

Chapter 30

I didn't want my family to know I was drinking the way I was, but I would ruin that plan big time. I was drinking with some friends at a house and they made me vodka and tang. I was not a vodka drinker because it just didn't taste good. However, I had never had it with tang. I downed the first one and it was smooth and sweet. The second one came right after. That is all I had before I left to go to a bar since the night was young. I had no idea how much alcohol was in those two drinks.

When I left my friend's house, I didn't feel like I had too much to drink and it was okay to drive. Right when I pulled into the parking lot of the bar, I felt really weird and almost had a drugged feeling, but told myself it must have been the alcohol. I went inside to call someone for a ride. The first place I called was the house I was at prior but no one answered. I called three times leaving messages. Still nothing. So, I called another friend and she said she was sleeping so I told her it was okay, I would call a cab.

Finally Free

I was really trying to be responsible. I spoke to the person at the door asking if they had a number for a cab but they were busy and told me to hold on. My body was not going to stand and wait. It walked right up to the bar and ordered a beer. I figured I would just go outside and wait for someone to come out who I knew and ask for a ride. I never took a sip of that beer.

I tucked that beer in my jacket and walked outside. I was sitting on the curb and because it was so early people weren't coming out, they were just going in. I certainly wasn't going to ask someone to leave a place they had just arrived. I waited outside for a long time. Alcoholic time, so maybe 20 minutes. I was feeling better and figured I could make it home. I put the beer in my coaster and off I drove.

Unfortunately, or fortunately, I didn't turn my lights on. Literally across the street from the bar is a gas station. I got pulled over for not having my lights on. Then the officer saw the open container and it was all over. He asked me to do the sobriety walking test. I quickly remembered my mom telling me when she got pulled over the officer told her to walk ten steps forward then ten steps back. She walked forward the ten steps and didn't turn around when walking the ten steps back. This was a funny story then but lost its humor in this moment. I refused to do the test because it's a small town and if someone saw me that would be too embarrassing.

Off to jail I went and you would think this would be the end of the drinking. Alcohol is like a hawk. It just waits quietly until you take that first drink and then swoops in and ruins things. I learned about hitting rock bottom but what I didn't know is that there can be many of them. I had never been in trouble like this and truly had no idea what was going to happen.

I had no control of what I was saying and I didn't care who I was saying it to. The one thing I never wanted to happen was to have to make that phone call to one of the grandmas who was watching Dakota. Worst moment in my whole life. Even though Dakota was still very young, the gig was up. I made the call and grandma assured me that Dakota would be fine.

The next morning, I was in a cell and there was another person in there with me. I put my whole head in an open shower to try to feel better. I started playing back the whole evening trying to figure out how two drinks got me to this point. I thought maybe I am getting older and alcohol isn't working like it used to. Then I thought, I will just stick to beer and Southern Comfort. Nothing too bad happened with those.

I truly tried to get a ride, but my mind had control over my body and I no longer had the choice of what I was doing. I never believed that to be true, even at that moment, but it was still happening. I met with an attorney and he asked, "Are you ready to go to treatment?" I looked up at him with my wet hair dripping down my wet shirt and said, "Sure, what's that?"

Chapter 31

In New Mexico at the time there was a saying, .08 gets you 28. That is 28 days in treatment or in jail. I talked with all the grandmas and we put a plan in place. Dakota would come see me every day that it was allowed which turned out to be five times a week. The treatment center was on a hill of some sort and it had a teepee not too far away. I was very positive about this adventure and I believed that it could fix the problem I had with alcohol.

Later I would learn it wasn't the alcohol that had the problem, it was the vessel it landed in. There were a couple of people from high school who I knew in treatment. They told me they thought I was a spy working for the police department. How I wish that would have been the case. I just wasn't someone to get into this kind of situation. I played it off for a few days that I possibly was a spy by moving my toothbrush toward them acting like there was a camera in it. I took it as a compliment and assured them I belonged there.

Finally Free

When Dakota would come visit, I would teach her how to play volleyball and play games. Everyone was really friendly and she was always entertained so she wouldn't have time to realize this was not actually a fun place. I would take her on walks and tell her how much I miss her and that I would be home very soon. We talked about school and what she was learning. My mom and grandparents were incredible during this horrible time. I truly felt so bad and embarrassed. I just should have been better.

By the time treatment was over it was kind of sad leaving. I had no desire to drink alcohol while I was there. We were so busy doing what I love, talking about other people's problems and supporting them the best I could. One of the counselors asked if I would like to come back and work there. He said I would have to stay sober for one year. I thought about it for half a second and said, "No but thanks so much". I did not want to work with a bunch of alcoholic adults who lied and kept going in and out of treatment. I was so arrogant during this time of my life and probably the most scared.

I just needed to get back to my life, my daughter and work. I had met a cool guy in treatment and he was getting out a couple days before me. The day I got out he came over and we drank together. Yep, that quick. It was exciting and wrong at the same time. The next day I picked up Dakota from my grandparents and things were back to normal. When I wasn't working, Dakota and I spent most of our time together. I didn't drink for a long time after that night. I really didn't want to drink anymore but I just couldn't completely stop.

Things were going pretty well for a long time. A friend introduced me to a really handsome guy and there was an immediate attraction.

My Story

We were so in love that Dakota had asked to call him dad, which he agreed. One time the three of us were out by the pool and Dakota was leaning down swishing the water from left to right. She was six at this point. He asked if she had ever had a spanking. Dakota looked over her shoulder and said, "Never have, never will". She had a killer sense of humor. Years later when she saw some home videos of herself, she made the comment that she was a smart alec. I only saw her as funny.

Things took a turn in the relationship. He informed me he was using drugs and this was a deal breaker, especially with Dakota. I moved into the counselor role pretty quickly which was an ultimate failure. I knew too much about codependency and I didn't need another thing to have to overcome. We were just too close and I loved him too much. To get away from this great guy I needed to make a move to another state. I was ready to get back out to California and this would be the perfect excuse. He died not too long after I moved away.

Chapter 32

One of the missionaries at church had parents who lived in Turlock California. I didn't know anyone there and had never even heard of it. I asked Dakota if she would like to move to California and she excitedly said yes. Dakota was doing great in school, had friends and family. So of course, the best thing for me to do was move her to a whole new life.

It was time for a new adventure. I finished college and got my Associates in Human Resources and a BS in Social Science. It wouldn't be too difficult to get a job with all of this knowledge. When we got to California, we moved right into the missionaries' parents' house. Do you have any idea how hard it was to drink in a church family home? So, of course the drinking slowed way down. I worked hard, went to church and did what I needed to do to get my own place.

We found an apartment across from Walmart. It was awesome and our neighbors quickly became friends with us. There were eight apartments in our section and we had a church family above us and one across and up the stairs. God was continuing to remind me that there is a better way if I would just stop trying to control my own destiny. Again, I saw this as balance. Drink with the drinking neighbors and go to church with the church neighbors. Keeping it simple.

We thrived in Turlock. Dakota had the best teachers and I got a job as a corrections officer for a juvenile hall in a couple cities over. We were driving in the neighborhood across from us and there was a house for rent. It was time for me to step up my parenting and get a house for my child. Not that she ever complained and I was totally comfortable in an apartment. I called the number on the sign and met with the owner. It had a pool and I was going to figure out a way to get this house.

After a few paychecks I was able to get the down payment and first month's rent. Dakota would have her first house. Dakota chose the colors for her room, Pepto-Bismol pink and purple. When she got back from visiting family, the room was painted and ready for her to decorate. Now all we needed was a dog. I have no idea where these thoughts came from and they were always out of the blue. Never a sincere pros and cons process. Thought then action.

Chapter 33

Dakota and I headed to the pound to get our first dog together. We took a dog to the area where you can get to know each other. Then they brought out Heidi. She was a greyhound and German shepherd mix. She was so hyper and she was huge. They said was just a puppy but she appeared to be full grown to me. We found our dog.

We were in line waiting to take her home and the lady asked if I had a kennel. I told her to hold the dog and I would run to Walmart to get one. By the time I got back there was a man with two boys in line and they had Heidi with them. I quickly went to the front of the line and told the lady that I got the kennel. She said she was sorry but she couldn't hold the dog. It had only been 30 minutes. This is where God was like, "Hey girls go pick a different dog". And Satan was like, "Get that dog no matter what".

Dakota started crying very quietly and I assured her we were going to get a dog just maybe not that one. The man looked back at us

Finally Free

as he was paying for Heidi. He told the lady, "It's their dog and we will find another one". The boys looked back unsure of what was happening and the wife stormed out the door. She has no idea what we saved her from. I told the man he didn't have to do that and thanked him. I had no idea that he was actually going to be doing us a favor if he bought the dog. If you are familiar with that "still small voice", listen to it.

When we first went home Heidi ran out back and jumped right into the pool. She was so awkward and didn't have any training at all. When I took her for walks, I had to wear my roller blades because she was so fast. One night we were out walking and she spotted a cat and took off. She wouldn't stop so I had to get down like I was sliding into first base. The problem was I was in the middle of the road so I got the deepest longest road burn ever.

I yelled for my mom and Dakota and went to the emergency room to get it cleaned out. I can still feel that scrub brush going across my shin. I could have really used a drink during that scrubbing. We loved Heidi so much but she was making my life very difficult. I would literally cry in my room after each thing she would destroy. You would think that I would have thought of taking her to a training class but I thought I could do it myself. After all, I had never trained a dog so of course I would be the best person to do this. No, my thought was that she would calm down as she got older and we spent more time with her.

Heidi needed so much attention and I worked swing shifts six days on three days off. My mom had moved in with us to help with Dakota but had no ability to train the dog. Heidi had torn up the fish pond and destroyed the backyard. I knew we had to let her go but I just didn't want to because I didn't want to take her back to the pound. I am not sure if it was pride, or fear that they would put her down.

I came home from work one afternoon and the neighbor pulled up with their little white dog. They had just gotten home from the vet and said that Heidi had attacked their dog. I ran into the backyard to be sure Heidi was there. She had jumped over the six-foot fence and there were drops of blood on the fence.

The neighbor's dog was not injured but they wanted Heidi out of the neighborhood or to be chained up. Chaining her up wasn't an option. I had tried that and she always got out. I had a conversation with the pound and they said they had a place for her. We pulled up to the gate in the back. It seemed like it took forever to open. Dakota and I were just crying and hugging her while she was jumping all around without a care in the world. We were bawling our eyes out telling her she would have a better life with new people. We followed up with the pound a few days later and Heidi had already been adopted. I don't know if that is just something they tell people or it really happened. Either way Dakota was okay believing Heidi was happy and safe.

Chapter 34

I was done drinking and I wanted to do what I could to ensure that I would be with Dakota forever as far as the church was concerned. In our church getting sealed in the temple guarantees you will be with your family forever. For me it was an outward showing of my commitment and I thought it would help me stay sober. I knew I would be with Dakota in Heaven no matter what but I needed to be active in the process.

This was more about following the system than me believing in it. God's will, not mine sort of thing. I already knew that I would be with her forever, or why would God have given her to me in the first place? I also had the complete understanding that she belonged to him and he was trusting me with her. When I spoke with the bishop, I learned that I would not be able to be sealed to Dakota unless I was married.

This gave me the perfect excuse to not ever go to the temple. I had gone when I was young to do baptisms for the dead so I wasn't ever that curious. No one was going to tell me that I had to be married to be sealed to my daughter for eternity. So, I just checked that off the list of things to do. We continued to go to church and I did my callings as they were offered to me. I did have a small resentment and wanted Dakota to experience other churches so she could make her own decision on what church she wanted to attend from her own experiences.

She was able to go to a church where they played music and clapped their hands. She was used to the quiet music and reverence. It was fun watching her look around and move her arms like she wanted to clap but just wasn't sure if it was appropriate. I told her she could clap if she wanted to. She said it just didn't feel right. I actually felt the same way. It didn't feel wrong as if the action was wrong, it was just not the same. Which is crazy because that seems to be where I would be most comfortable.

The next church had incense so we didn't stay in there too long. I really didn't know much about any other churches but she got to see that there was more than just our church and she had a choice. The next Sunday in church it felt right to be there. I didn't have to agree with the way everything was set up but I knew that this was the place for me and Dakota felt the same. I still felt that I didn't fit in, but there was something that kept me involved and I wasn't going to fight it. I was never brave enough to get too far away, or maybe my faith was stronger than I realized.

Chapter 35

Dakota continued to do great in school. She had awesome friends and participated in many sports like soccer, softball and cheer. She was really good in all sports but her passion was for cheerleading. This is where she would find her true lifelong friends and begin to figure out who she is and what goals she wanted to set for herself. I was doing well at the corrections facility and loved the people I worked with.

There was only one guy who worked there that went to the same church and he lived it to the fullest. He used to read his scriptures on the night shift while I was watching movies. This was allowed because it was a graveyard shift and all the kids were sleeping so we just had to do our 15-minute checks. I managed to get my master's degree while working in corrections but also found people who drank like me.

Dina was the one I hung out with the most. She was a single mom as well and she knew everything about this job and how it worked.

Finally Free

She was firm but fair and honestly just a "bad ass". She had one daughter and our girls were the same age. Her daughter was more of a "tomboy" than mine. We had a lot in common so it was easy to hang out and do nothing sometimes. We were both boy crazy and super picky for the one we wanted for the long term. This kept us single for many years and probably saved many men.

Working in corrections with minors was very emotionally draining at times. I tried to come up with new ideas to help the kids realize their potential. We put together an Olympics, and held it out in the rec yard. We also did gingerbread houses with graham crackers, frosting and popsicle sticks. My friend Marty did not think this was going to be successful. To his surprise the kids were so good at it, and made houses with garages.

Marty was my best guy friend. He was very much into baseball, very kind and way smarter than me. He would be sure we got back all of the sticks so no one would make a weapon out of them. I really didn't like the environment but I did feel like I was helping the kids so I stayed there for seven years. I was getting really good at controlled drinking. I got back to my workout routine, traveled a lot with Dakota and was making more money than I had ever made before. It was time to buy my own home instead of renting.

I found a house on the other side of town. It was in a cul-de-sac and the neighbors were very nice. Dina and Marty had both encouraged this so I could have an investment. I had no idea what I was doing. It was a three bedroom and I put in wood floors, new carpet and new toilets. We put in new grass for a trampoline in the backyard and concrete on one half of it for an above ground swimming pool.

My Story

I even had the neighbor put in the hammock I had always wanted. One of the greatest things about having your own yard to work in is being able to drink while you're mowing the lawn. I was learning to fix sprinkler heads and use different products to make my grass look as good as the neighbors. I was a home owner and life couldn't be any better. I had gotten a job at the local gym teaching water aerobics so we could have a free membership. Dakota would go to work with me and anytime the class didn't know the exercise, she would jump up on the deck and show them the moves. I remember racing her around the tennis court when she was in high school. When she beat me, I had to play it off like I let her win. She knew the truth.

I had gotten compliments on Dakota and my parenting skills considering how I was raised. Some friends said, "I can't believe you're such a good mom considering your parents". Although that was rude, I took it as a compliment. I don't think my mom was a bad parent, I think she just preferred working. I would just tell myself to do better and show up no matter what. Show up, be open to any conversations, be a good example, work hard, listen and most of all have fun. This is why it was important to be on my best behavior when Dakota was around. When she wasn't I would be irresponsible within means and behave badly. I liked both sides of me for many years.

Dakota started hanging out with her friends more often once she was in high school. This left me to have more time to myself. My really good drinking friends were Gloria, Julissa, Dina and Marty. If one of them was busy another would be available. I didn't ever have to drink alone. We were moving past the going out to the bar stage into drinking at each other's houses.

Finally Free

During this time, I was really not wanting to drink anymore. As this story goes this is a common occurrence and I meant it every time. I was going to be transitioning from working in corrections to working as a social worker. I wanted to be sure I was no longer drinking when starting this new job. I needed to be focused and ready to learn new things. I started going to 12-step meetings again and was getting some days together without alcohol. I instantly felt the difference physically. I had more energy and my guilt was lifted. When I went to church, I didn't have that lingering feeling of how imperfect I was. Things were looking up.

Chapter 36

My grandma, who had never been sick in my life, was now in the hospital. She was in her late 90s and in great health. When I got the call from my mom, I did not hesitate to let my boss know that I had to take some time off. It was a new job but there was no way I wasn't going to go home and be with my grandma. Being the awesome man he was, he told me to take the time I needed and for me to just let him know what was happening and when I would be returning.

I had been going to meetings regularly and had 95 days sober. My mentor said I wouldn't drink over my grandma being sick. I would drink over a broken shoelace. I didn't believe it when she said that and boy, was she wrong. I went to the hospital straight away when we got to New Mexico. When I went into the room and saw that my grandma was so frail, I just wanted to cry. But I went over and sat on her bed and made some jokes. She was so happy to see me and Dakota. I took the first shift staying with her while Dakota went home with my mom to get some rest from our trip. A couple days later it was my turn to take a break. And that break could have been my breaking point.

I was walking around the house looking at all of her things and praying that she didn't die. She was the head of our tiny family. She was always there for every one of us no matter what we needed. She would do anything to help us out and never sugar-coated things. She taught me to be strong and get things done. She never felt sorry for herself or complained about her life. She taught me to hold my heart close to my chest as well as my money. She was a full on Republican and when we were in her house, we all became Republicans whether we were or not. I always respected her and she was so smart, strong and beautiful. She just couldn't leave us, not yet, she still had so much to teach Dakota.

As I went to the refrigerator, I saw the little Tupperware containers with words written in black permanent marker. "Peas, mashed potatoes, beets." When I opened the containers there would be literally two or three bites in each one. She always tried to give me powdered milk by disguising it in a regular milk carton. When I called her out on it, she just started laughing and told me it's the same as other milk.

She made the best cheese toast in the broiler with grits and had the funniest laugh with a snort. She chewed her food all the way before swallowing. She told me to chew it 20 times before swallowing for better digestion. I was remembering my whole life walking through the house and I just couldn't lose her. I had to get out of the house and asked if Jack's son wanted to go see a movie with me. He didn't want to leave his tv and beer.

My Story

I thought about finding a meeting but I chose to go to a movie instead. I figured I would walk since it wasn't too far. On my way there was a convenience store and I would grab some candy and a Dr. Pepper to sneak into the theater. I grabbed a small bottle of Southern Comfort and some candy and headed out.

Chapter 37

At the movie theater I ordered a medium diet coke. I didn't think about anything else but getting to my seat and mixing this drink. It was the Liam Neeson film, "The Grey". I had no idea what the storyline was about. It was definitely the wrong movie to watch at this depressing juncture. I was crying quietly and there was hardly anyone in the theater. As I was walking home, I was feeling better but still very sad. I knew I had to hold it together for the rest of the family. A couple days later we brought my grandma home.

Hospice had set up a hospital bed in the living room which is never a good sign. I was determined to get her better and was not anywhere near acceptance of the situation. I loaded her up in the car and took her for walks down at the river as much as she could handle. She liked seeing all of the veteran flags, memorials, ducks and listening to the water. We talked about my grandpa Tex and she wondered what he was doing in Heaven. A couple missionaries came over to give her a blessing. She was a hard-core Baptist and would always

Finally Free

ask me if I was still going to that Mormon church. We were waiting for her to say something crazy. Instead, she got a huge smile and said they were very nice and thanked them for the blessing.

The last week I was there, Grandma was still talking and making jokes but I could tell she wasn't going to turn the corner. She had stopped eating and drinking and she continued to lose weight. She talked about her sisters who had already passed and sometimes her breath was so faint we thought she was gone. Her body was just so tired. She had carried a whole lifetime and it was time to turn it over to God. Dakota was by her side every day giving her foot rubs, reading to her and rubbing lotion on her tan, weathered body. Grandma looked me in the eye, pointed her finger and said, "You have to get things in order".

We all just looked at each other not really understanding what she meant. We didn't know until after her death that her current husband's son would steal the house from under us. I had to get back to my new job and Dakota had to get back to school. My mom was able to be by her side and called me with the news that she had passed just a couple weeks later. Dakota and I were at a breast cancer marathon when I got the call. We quickly went home and I got in the shower and cried like I had never cried in my life even to this day. The legacy was gone and now it was my turn to be there for everyone. I would do my best to listen without judgment and never take sides within the family. We would stick together and get through anything. That would be the goal.

Chapter 38

I had a work trip with the new job in Lake Tahoe and free alcohol was included. My new coworkers were very excited about this, I was nervous. Since I drank that day while visiting my grandma, I had to start my sober days over again. I was going to meetings from time to time but did not continue working with that mentor and was not willing to get another one. I was "not drinking" and doing just fine. We arrived in Lake Tahoe and it took about one hour before my drink was on.

I didn't know these people very well so I wanted to make a good impression. There were some who drank like me and others who drank like normal people. And only one who didn't drink at all. I certainly wasn't going to be like her. It was a successful, fun trip and there was no drama that had to do with me. I thought maybe I was able to drink now and not have anything bad happen. That sneaky little devil reared its ugly head a few months later.

Finally Free

This was definitely a party group of people I was working with. One of the supervisors was having a party at her house. Everyone was getting pretty hammered. I had brought my bike so I wouldn't be tempted to drink and drive. The party was winding down and I got on my bike to go home. I lived pretty far and if I had to walk it would probably have taken two hours. I hopped on my bike and off I went.

Just a block down the road my bike just fell over. I picked it up, started riding and it fell over again. I pushed it away from me while holding the handlebars with my arms straight out. I literally said out loud, "Are you really looking at this bike like it's the bike's fault you can't stay up?" I had never had this happen before and it was really kind of scary. I ended up walking the rest of the way home thinking about going back to meetings, getting a mentor and getting back to being sober. Or I could just walk from now on or get a ride or drink at home.

We had been in Turlock for about 12 years and it was too far from San Diego. We wanted to get closer to the beach and this so-called investment of a house needed to be cashed out. Again, no idea what I was doing and totally got screwed on the sale. Dakota was thinking about colleges, jobs and what she wanted to do after she graduated. She had gotten her cosmetology license while in high school and I had experience in jobs with the state, teaching and social work. Once Dakota graduated, we made the move.

Chapter 39

We were going to stay with family until we found jobs or Dakota decided what college she was going to go to. I had no idea that this move would literally be the most transformational move in my life thus far. I had exactly 10,000 dollars in savings. I paid off my car and I would have no payments or bills left behind. We had never traveled with a U-Haul before but I had an SUV and was told it wasn't too bad. When we got to Carlsbad, we unloaded our things into a storage facility. We got a room set up which we shared in my family's house. This was going to be very temporary.

Dakota found a job using her cosmetology license and was doing very well. She also took a second job at Victoria's Secret for the discounts. I applied at many places and was not getting any interviews or call backs. I started freaking out because we needed to find a place to live so we could start our life here. Not realizing our lives had already started the day we were born and they didn't need to keep waiting to start again. I didn't want to take a job at a fast-food place because I felt that would be going backwards. I had two degrees and no jobs were coming my way.

I was still drinking but it didn't feel like before. Now it felt like I was thinking about stopping way more than I was actually drinking. I was asking God, "If I stop will you let me have a job?" I just didn't think I was doing anything wrong to deserve this. Later I would learn that if God gave me what I deserved it may not be such a good thing. One morning I was walking with some ladies from church. I was listening to them talk about activities that were coming up and plans for their vacations. All I could think about was getting to my car and going to a meeting. There was this big world around me moving forward and I was on a hamster wheel going nowhere.

I said goodbye to the ladies and jumped into my SUV. I sat for a minute or two then out loud I said, "What are you waiting for, just do it. God, please remove the desire to drink alcohol." I looked up the hotline for a recovery group on my phone. A kind voice was on the other end. Immediately I felt relieved and said, "I am in Carlsbad, where do I go?"

I headed toward the beach and found the meeting in a small church off one of the main roads in town. I listened to everyone speak and there was one lady who stood out. Her name was Jennifer. Jennifer was real, smiled when she talked and was super energetic. After the meeting I asked her to be my mentor. We went outside and sat on a bench to talk a little more. I gave her a little history and she told me she would work with me. It was a good fit and off we went.

My Story

Now that I had a mentor and was six days sober, I was sure that God would give me a job. I continued to apply and nothing was coming my way. I realized that my job was to go to meetings every day and be grateful to be sober. Appreciate my health and that I had no debt. Though things were changing it felt like crap and I totally didn't get it. Later I thought about if God had given me a great job would I have stayed sober? If I am honest, I know that I would not.

Chapter 40

It was time that Dakota and I moved out so we had to come up with something ASAP. Dakota found a room to rent with three or four other girls and we got her moved in very quickly. I loaded up my car with nowhere to go, except a meeting. I shared my situation in front of everyone and a woman after the meeting came up and talked to me. She said, "I have a couch". I said, "I will take it". Her name was Dee. She had over 20 years of sobriety at the time and was an angel sent from God just for me.

Dee had lived by herself long enough to know she really liked it. It was a big deal for her to let me in her home and it was a big deal for me to ask. It was very humiliating even being in this situation and she made it feel like I was exactly where I needed to be. But I had heard enough stories in recovery and this was nothing compared to how it could be. So, I moved into gratitude very quickly.

Finally Free

One day I was feeling a lot of self-pity and anger that nothing was working out. I walked into the grocery store and I heard this man's voice say, "Excuse me?" In my mind I thought geez what do you want, and as I turned around it was a man in a wheelchair with no legs and one arm. He wanted me to hand him something off the shelf. I looked up and said, "Seriously, I can't feel sorry for myself for one minute". I got the item then he asked me how much sugar was in it. We talked for a bit and I was cured of my selfishness.

Dee was a very busy person but she always checked in with me to be sure I was doing okay. She had activities with school, recovery, friends and community engagements. I loved her energy and how kind she was. She had this pleasant tone about her when she asked me to do things for her that made it impossible to feel annoyed. She had these palm trees out front and they kept dropping these little sticker balls. I can't tell you how many of those balls I swept up but I never complained even in my mind with no one around.

But I did wonder, "Why doesn't she hire the guy to come and chop those off so she won't have these balls everywhere?" She was also particular about her shower curtain being pulled closed after I showered. This way it wouldn't get moldy. All the years I had a shower curtain and never had a problem with mold. I completely understood but I thought for a second, holy crap is she going to follow me around this house telling me how to do things every day. This was not the case and I am grateful I didn't make a stink about the curtain. This would become a lifelong joke between us.

Chapter 41

Dee and I became friends and after a few days trust was built and she gave me my own key. Before that, I had to wait for her to get home and leave when she left even if I didn't have anywhere to go. These were the things that kept me sober, believe it or not.

I was parked in front of a recovery meeting, where I had met Jennifer, when I got a call for a job at the YMCA in La Jolla. I was so grateful until I heard him say, "I am sorry we can't start you out with more with all of your experience". My heart kind of dropped but I told myself it's more than what you have now. But then he said $9.50 an hour. I started silently crying and couldn't help but get quiet. He assured me I would get a raise very quickly. I just sucked up my feelings and what I really wanted to say and responded with, "Yes, that's fine".

I went home and let Dee know that I got a job. I could now give her some money each month for letting me stay. Dee was very happy for me. Dee reminded me that prior to me moving in she had someone coming to stay with her in a few months and I would need to find another place to stay. It was coming up and again, I had to find a place to live. I had met many people in the program and they were my best resources. It just felt safe being with people in recovery.

I found a place to stay with a couple guys in recovery. They were gay so there was no temptation of trying to start a relationship or anything inappropriate. One of them was a boxer so me and some friends went to see him fight. I stayed there for a week then moved to an apartment that my new boss had available for the next month. He stayed with his girlfriend most of the time so his apartment was empty. His lease would be up in a month so I would have to move out again. Three different places in such a short period of time. I would pack everything up and empty everything out. Even though this was a very difficult situation I was still so happy and felt so free. I felt like an adventurer and a homeless person all in one. I have to admit though, it was getting a little exhausting.

I decided that I would live in my car. It was an SUV so there was plenty of space. Since I worked at the YMCA, I could get up early, work out, shower, work, go run errands in the day and come back to the parking lot to sleep. My work outfit was just shorts and a t-shirt so I never had to dress up. For church I just wore a top and skirt and flip flops. I had no bills and no responsibilities to anyone but myself.

I heard somewhere that I am exactly where I am supposed to be. I did wonder why God wanted me here, in my car, with limited funds and a job a teenager could do. What was I getting punished for? I

My Story

was literally doing everything right. I was humble and grateful. My attitude was good and I was helping others. I worked hard and had very few material things. I was sober and doing meetings every day and meeting with my mentor to work the steps. What was the miracle they say to wait for? Could it be all of the above? Would I feel this free if I wasn't exactly where I was at this very moment?

Chapter 42

I went to the welfare department to see what kind of housing I might qualify for or any better paying jobs. There was a halfway house for women but I didn't qualify because I was too young. The other house failed because I wasn't a chronic alcoholic. I went to the homeless shelter to see what that was about. I parked my car far away because I didn't want people to think I didn't belong because of my car. I was thinking if I could just get a meal or two a day, I could use the money I was making to save for my own place.

I stood in line with all the others waiting for my turn. This was the place that was supposed to help homeless people find jobs, food, shelter and showers. I was willing to try anything. When it was my turn, the guy actually said, "What are you doing here?" I told him I was there to talk to a counselor to find out what services might be available. He gave me a number, told me the shower schedule and when meals were provided. I waited against the wall in this long hallway that came out to a waiting area with old furniture and a T.V.

Finally Free

Outside the door there was a huge trash bag full of donuts. People were just digging in there grabbing a handful of old broken donuts. Not even picky about what kind they would get, imagine that. I was standing with my back up against the wall looking at all of these homeless people wandering around looking so broken and so sad. I looked up and quietly whispered, "God, please give them all peace". I left the building telling myself that I was not at this point yet, and that there had to be another way. I had collected some bars of soap and toothpaste that I brought when I moved so I dropped them off at the front before driving away.

The next resource I used was the church. The bishop knew a man whose mom had just moved out of her home because she was ill and could not take care of it by herself. When I drove up to the house, I passed a golf course and huge homes everywhere. The house was condemned and was waiting to be demolished because it was no longer safe to live in. To me it was a castle. It was at the very top of the long hill into the center of La Jolla.

The son had the electricity and water turned on for me. I mostly showered at work because I didn't want to use too much hot water. It smelled like an old house that had been sitting without any care. Her things were still in it so I stayed in one room and only used the kitchen as needed. But it was mine for at least a month. I made friends with the lawyers next door and learned that many people in that neighborhood rented out their basement to travel nurses and students. Secrets of the rich, I thought.

One day the wife came over and she was looking in the house to be sure I was going to have what I needed. She probably just wanted to be a little snoopy but I liked having the company. When we got to the bedroom where I was sleeping, she noticed some brown dust on the sheet. She asked if I knew what that was. I said, "Dust?" "No, it's termite feces." I found another room to sleep in. I would walk down to La Jolla almost every day to go to a meeting and to work out. It took about an hour and a half. I went to some great meetings there and continued to meet with Jennifer.

Chapter 43

Dee had called me a few months later and asked where I was living. I had misunderstood her when she said I needed to move out. I thought I couldn't live with her anymore but she only meant the person was there for a visit. She quickly offered for me to come back to the house. I was so happy to be back with her. She was such a great example to me and we had a true friendship. Doors kept closing on me as far as a job, to the point that my mentor started praying for me. She told me she said, "God please give this girl a break".

I was settling into my new life as a recovering alcoholic. It was simple and so rewarding. I took a second job nannying for a surgeon. He was very sweet and liked how I was with the kid at the school. He had a boy and a girl. They were Jewish and he did his best to teach him some traditions. It was interesting watching these kids in this beautiful home with divorced rotating parents. Instead of having the kids go to other houses the parents came to this house and rotated themselves.

Finally Free

Never again did I act like I know what goes on in the beautiful ritzy houses. They are just like anyone else. He would often offer me a glass of wine with dinner and I would let him know I don't drink. I knew I was done drinking but rejecting the wine assured me that the day I asked for the desire to be removed, it truly was.

It was time for a new adventure. Dakota had met some really great friends at church and they convinced her to apply for Brigham Young University Idaho. I had wanted to go to Brigham Young University Utah back in the day but I had no idea how to even start that process. I think my friend Donna actually did everything for me when I attended New Mexico State. The school Dakota wanted to attend was in Idaho and neither of us had any idea what Idaho was about. Dakota and I were walking up from the beach toward her place. She asked me if I was coming with her. It didn't even need to be asked, I was always ready for change.

I did need to run this by my mentor because I only had seven months of sobriety and it is suggested not to make big changes at that point, but I was feeling pretty confident. I also talked it over with Dee because she had so much time and would be honest with me. They both agreed that if Dakota was going, I would be going no matter what they said so they gave the approval. We went to the storage and loaded up what we wanted to take. Each time we unloaded the storage we tended to let a little more go. By the time we got to Idaho we had a smaller U-Haul and not very much in the car.

Dakota and I had looked on the map to see the best place for me to live since she was going to live on the campus. It was between Idaho Falls and Pocatello. As we headed out of town, we talked about visiting some people along the way. We had a distant relative in Utah as well as an old high school friend. As we got closer to Utah, we realized we did not have the appropriate clothing for this weather. Luckily, we had both been skiers so we had jackets. Our gloves were more for a light breeze not snow. We stopped at the mall and took some pictures outside in the snow. The air was so crisp and clean. It was so beautiful and so cold.

We met distant relatives that we found on Ancestry a while back. We had some fun conversations about people we both knew and they brought out some photos. Dakota was excited to see where she got her height of 5'1" from. They didn't offer for us to stay so we went on to our friend's house on the other side of Utah. As we were driving into Eagle Mountain, we could see all of the churches and a couple temples along the way. Dakota looked over at me and said, "Oh my gosh, we're so going to get married". Then we both laughed. In my mind I thought, yes, YOU are. I had no desire to get married. I was loving my new sober life and had plenty to do, in finding my new tribe.

Chapter 44

We had a great visit with our friends and stayed the night. She owned a restaurant called, "Six Sisters". Before we left the next day I confirmed, via text, that the place we had lined up was good to go. The lady responded that it was and said the key would be under the grate near the front door. We were getting closer to Pocatello and I couldn't even see the city. It was covered in snow. The trailer was pulling my car left and right due to the wind being so strong and the ground so slick. We saw a sign that said, "Trucks Pull Over". I wasn't sure why until I saw a semi turned on its side. We just looked at each other and thought, where the heck had we moved to?

Dakota was not able to get into her dorm until the next day so we headed to the place we would stay for the night. The key was somewhere under the snow and impossible to find. The lady would not return my text so we found a small business across the street to warm up in and figure something out. We got back online to

Finally Free

find a place. It was close and it was just for the night. When we got there, it was very dark in the house. The girl looked like she was in her 20s and wasn't very personable.

She showed us the room with a mattress on the floor. There was also a dog there which I was very allergic to. You're probably wondering why we didn't get a hotel. I was always so frugal and Dakota was just a victim of that. We got a little sleep but as soon as morning hit, we were out of there. I left some money on the kitchen table with a note thanking her for letting us stay the night.

I took Dakota to her dorm and it was beautiful. The campus was amazing and her roommates were very cool. I wanted to stay with her but I needed to find a place for myself. I got back on Craigslist and found a trailer that was available. The owner worked out of town a lot and needed someone to watch his dogs. Again, I am allergic but they were outside dogs. He warned me it needed some work and was dirty. I thought to myself, that's okay, I am sober and grateful so it will be fine. First, I needed to get this stuff into storage. I grabbed Dakota and we found a storage place very close to her school for a great price.

As we were unloading everything it was so cold that we had to keep jumping in the car to warm our hands. We looked at the temperature and it was -7. I asked her, "Once it's below zero why even count anymore?" I jumped back out and told Dakota to stay in the car. As I was jumping over the trailer hitch my shoelace got caught, and down I went, flat on my back. I was yelling for Dakota but she had the music turned up. I just lay there thinking, what the hell am I doing here?

My Story

Due to the cold our hands would get frozen and it took multiple trips to storage. I made it to the trailer and the owner's ex-wife was there with a key. When I walked in it smelled like dead animals and dog feces. There were beer cans and bottles everywhere and kids and adults clothing. I walked to the bathroom and heard dogs barking. I had no idea how many were in there and I wasn't going to open the door to find out. One of the two little boys that came with their mom ran past me to let the dogs out.

They were huge but acted like puppies. The other little boy got the dog food and just poured it all over the floor. The dogs got occupied quickly with the food and gave me a chance to get away. So many thoughts were screaming through my head. Call CPS, I can do this, call CPS, I can do this, I just need some cleaning supplies. Then the best thought came to my head; call your mentor. I told the ex-wife I was going to go get some cleaning supplies. I was in Walmart when I called my mentor. I told her the situation. She said, "Leave Walmart, go back to the house, put the keys on the counter and get the hell out of there". I was so relieved.

Chapter 45

It was New Year's so I knew there would be a meeting going on in this city, population over 60,000. The one I found was like walking into a bar. People were talking loudly and kids were running around during the meeting while someone was sharing. Others were on their cell phones not giving respect to the person talking at the podium in the front of the room. But hey, these were my people so I figured I'd take a seat and learn.

After the meeting I asked a lady if she knew of anyone looking for a roommate. She then asked me if I was on probation. I said no and thanked her for her help. Would I really be able to stay sober in this town? It was too cold to sleep in my car so I reached out to the church and they put me in a hotel for a few days so I could figure out where I needed to go when the sun was up. The next day I woke up and I was in Idaho Falls. It was magnificent. I had always loved the snow and to see so much of it was amazing. It was a brand-new day in a brand-new city.

Finally Free

I should have stopped using Craigslist but I thought I would give it one more shot. I found a lady who was my age, went to my church and sounded okay on the phone. Again, I loaded everything into my car and headed to her apartment. Not even three days later she told me this may not work out because she didn't want me to see her have panic attacks. Before she could even finish the sentence, I was loading up my car.

Idaho Falls was only about 20 minutes from Dakota. Close but not too close so she could build her own life on campus and I could take her shopping and do fun things when she was available. Idaho Falls didn't have my bank so I headed to Wells Fargo because that is where my car loan had been. I talked to a man named Chris and told him my living situation. Squeaky wheel syndrome is what I have when desperate. He told me about a friend of his who was looking to rent a room. She worked for an insurance company and car insurance was next on my list of things to do. He called her and set up an appointment.

She was a super nice lady, married and lived near the airport. This was their first time renting a room so we took everything very slow and talked through the process. We had things in common and built a friendship very quickly. I went to the unemployment office and was able to get a job as a substitute teacher. This allowed me to pay for the room and continue looking for a better job. I found my ward in church and made friends very quickly. Since I was sober and in a new town, I had a fresh start and could be whoever I wanted to be. Turns out I was still me, I just didn't drink, and that was okay.

Chapter 46

There was much to learn in recovery and I was open to it all. I found some other meetings to attend in Idaho Falls. The one I really liked seemed to have some women with some long-term recovery and I needed a mentor. The first lady I asked was Sally. She said she traveled a lot and would not be able to meet with me. I was kind of taken aback because I thought you had to say yes if someone asked you to mentor them. I had so much to learn. No is an answer too. We continue to be friends to this day. The second lady I asked wasn't sure what to do with me since I had already been through the steps. We tried it out for a few months but she was just too busy so I let her go. She was relieved. We're still friends as well.

Living sober can be really challenging. I was more judgmental and sensitive sober than I was when I was drinking. Things seemed to matter much more and I felt everything. As I worked on building my recovery network, I met a newcomer named Perry. I told him about a dance that was coming up and said that he should go. He walked into the dance with hands in his pockets just scared shitless. It was great.

I couldn't take it anymore so I went over to talk with him. We set up a time to go hiking and that is when I realized this was going to be my Idaho guy friend. He was single as well and I knew there wasn't going to be an issue with dating since we were both so new. After all he was a newcomer and I had two years. I was a professional. We met up for a hike and became instant friends. I shared with him my experience and helped him connect with other people in the program.

I invited another girlfriend of mine into our hiking crew and then another. It was mostly me, Perry and Dawn. We hiked the most amazing mountains in Wyoming. We talked about life, recovery, the past, the present and the future. Dawn had a few more years than me so she was the expert in recovery. Of course, I say these things jokingly. No matter how much time someone has we all only have today. It was just easy to be with Perry and he was a good example of what a husband could be. He was on a journey finding his place in the workforce as well so we supported each other in this. There was never a time where the conversation stalled or was uninteresting. He cared about Dakota and was very thoughtful. I am grateful for all of my relationships with people in recovery.

One night I was hanging out in a church parking lot after visiting with some friends and heard this guy talking. He was really funny and he was talking about losing his virginity to prostitutes and sitting in his underwear drunk in his front yard and his mom yelling at the neighbors, "Leave him alone, he's an artist". He was hilarious and

My Story

I couldn't look away. I knew I was going to be friends with him. In recovery it was recommended to me not to get in a relationship until I was at least two years sober. I had just over two years and still didn't want a relationship.

This guy's name was Cory and we were just going to be friends. The conversation he was having was wrapping up and I quickly went over to talk to him. I found out later he was terrified when I came up to him. I told him how funny he was and he said I was funny too. I told him we should do a podcast together. He said he was on the radio and that is why he moved to Idaho Falls. I didn't believe him nor did I know what that meant. I just kept talking and he kept being funny. It was March and really cold in the parking lot. We kept talking as we walked to our cars that were pretty far apart.

It was one of those conversations you wanted to continue but it was too cold and neither person was going to make a suggestion to go somewhere else. As I kept getting closer to my car he said, "Do you like Mackenzie River Pizza or Stockman's?" I said excitedly, "I love Mackenzie River Pizza". I opened my door and jumped in my car to roll down the window. As I jumped in, I split my pants. He then yelled, "I have to go by my apartment because I have coupons". "Awesome, see you there," I said. As I was driving, I thought, oh great he is cheap and poor. Then I thought, how cool is it that he admitted he has coupons. We got to the pizza place and I let him know I split my pants and we laughed.

We got a table in the bar area. There wasn't even a thought about it. He was six years sober at the time and neither of us were triggered by this environment. We talked about everything from religion, how we were raised, to mommy and daddy issues, work and things we like to do for fun. He really became hyper focused on the fact that I was a member of the church he was so interested in learning more about. He told me he wanted to go into the temple and he had a plan to make a fake card to get in.

He wanted me to introduce him to the Prophet. I guess he thought we all just knew each other and I could just call him up. I let him know the bishop was as far as I could take him and the rest was up to him. We talked for hours and it was getting late. I didn't want him to know how much I was really liking talking to him. This was changing from friendship to something else I had not experienced and it was freaking me out. He was much younger than I was and there was no way I was going to pull off a Demi and Ashton situation. Before we parted ways, I told him we were going to another meeting the next day in another town. He agreed to come.

We decided to all go get something to eat before the meeting. Cory put himself in the corner next to the wall. I mean right up against the wall. I didn't say anything because he already looked uncomfortable. At the end of each meeting, we held hands for the closing. I placed myself next to him so that I could feel what his hand was like. They were not the hands of a construction worker. In fact, they were the softest man hands I had ever felt. I thought to myself, so this is what a DJ's hand feels like.

We made plans again and continued to talk every day. He took me to concerts and I got to meet country music singers like Garth Brooks, Clint Black, Chase Rice, etc. I would post pictures of me and the superstars on Facebook to show off a little to my friends. Dating

My Story

a DJ gave me access to so many cool events including concerts, tractor pulls, state fairs, etc. Dating someone younger was very difficult for the first year. I had more of an issue than he did of course because I was older. Luckily, I am young at heart and he has pretty poor vision. We are so different and that is what makes us a great match. He lets me be who I am and he is who he is even when I try to change him.

Chapter 47

I was substitute teaching still so my schedule was very flexible. Almost too flexible. I knew this freedom couldn't last because I needed a job that provided insurance and stability. One evening before a meeting I was sitting out front with Cory. I told him I had something to talk to him about and made it sound serious. I said, "I got a job at Vocational Rehabilitation". A friend from church told me about her friend who worked for Vocational Rehabilitation. I had no idea what this place was or what I would be doing. I called to set up a time to come by and meet the owner. I learned that it was a state job and I would be working with students with disabilities in helping them get ready for work after high school. It turned out to be so much more than that.

I had an assistant named Amy, who was really my trainer, friend, organizer and the knower of all things related to VR. The majority of people I worked with were nondrinkers which made this transition very easy. My schedule allowed me to go to my meetings, work with others in recovery and network with the community and outreach programs. I learned to be more patient and tolerant of others. It took the full three years but I could feel the changes and I was maturing in the necessary areas. My supervisors were very patient with my enthusiasm for wanting things to go the way I wanted them to go. Working with people with disabilities gave me a new perspective on what a disability is and how we can help each person have a quality of life if they are willing. At some point we will all have a disability before we die and it was an honor to have this experience with VR and the clients and families.

Cory and I were moving into the next level of a relationship. We hadn't been intimate and both of us agreed this was probably why we were still together. We took a full nine months to get to know each other. We both talked to our mentor about moving in together and getting married. With some hesitation, our mentors agreed. They were older and had seen many recovery couples' relationships fail when their program was neglected. They gave us the go ahead and we started making a plan to move into his apartment.

We met with the bishop and told him what our plan was. He really thought it would be better if we got a civil marriage so we wouldn't be tempted to have sex. We tried to convince him we were not going to but he did not sway. Cory and I had some thinking to do. Neither of us were in a hurry to get married but if he wanted to go inside the temple and I wanted to be sealed to my daughter this was the way to go. There were many more conversations and we both knew we wanted to be together so why not.

My Story

Cory is not a traditional guy as far as weddings and holidays so I knew I would have to take the lead on this. We agreed that I would buy an inexpensive ring and give it to him then he could ask me whenever he was ready. Neither of us was in a hurry but for some reason the universe decided to kick everything into gear.

While I was building this relationship with Cory, Dakota was building hers with Ian. Dakota and Ian met at BYUI. Dakota was visiting me at the house where I was renting a room near the airport. As we were walking out, she told me she was going to marry Ian. When I looked at her, I did my best to not talk and not freak out.

This was such a bad time for me, I thought. I wasn't making enough money to put on a wedding and I couldn't get engaged now because Dakota would be getting engaged. I just smiled and asked if she was sure she didn't want to wait until she finished college. She said, "No, I am sure that whatever I want to do in the future he can just do it with me". I knew by her tone that this was going to happen no matter what and she was happy.

Then she informed me that she wanted to get married in the La Jolla Temple in San Diego. That was always my favorite temple and I'd told myself if I ever got married that was where I would do it. I was finally going to go to the La Jolla Temple, not as a bride, but as a mom, to the most beautiful person I know. Luckily Cory wanted to be married in the Salt Lake Temple and there was no changing his mind. At this point in my life, it just didn't matter to me. I was more concerned about making the commitment to go through the temple no matter which one it was.

Finally Free

I took the temple classes while Cory was taking classes to join the church. He studied much better than I did and came up with some great questions for the missionaries. Everything was going pretty smoothly for all four of us. Talk about things happening in sobriety beyond my wildest dreams. This was in no way on my bucket list and all of a sudden, this perfect stranger walks this path with me with no hesitation.

Chapter 48

Dakota and I headed to San Diego for a visit. Ian's family came and we all went on a hike called Potato Chip. When we got up to the actual Potato Chip Ian, Dakota and myself went to the top. Everyone else was standing down below looking up our way. As I was standing there, unbeknownst to me, Ian knelt down. I quickly ducked out of the way onto another rock. The family on the ground knew this was happening but I did not.

Ian thought he had texted me but after searching for this text on his phone he realized he did not and was very apologetic. I was so happy and sad at the same time. This was my only child, the love of my life, my friend, my Dakota. Prior to this hike Ian and I were driving together to see his brother and he asked me for Dakota's hand and I said yes. But I still really didn't know much about him. I knew enough at that time to feel comfortable to let her go but not comfortable enough to live too far away from them.

Finally Free

As we were all walking back down the hill, I told them I would catch up because I had to use the restroom. When I finished there was no one within my visibility. This went on for quite a while as I walked down the hill. I just saw my daughter get engaged and now she was just gone. I had never felt so alone in my life. I said to God out loud, "This is it; this is how I am letting her go and now I am truly alone?" Immediately I said, "You have God and will never be alone". This brought much comfort but I was still butt hurt that no one came back to walk with me. This is a downfall of being too independent.

Cory and I had decided to go see my mom in Cortez, Colorado. She lived in a modest trailer and worked at Walmart full time. It was around the holidays and it was pretty cold there. Our visit was short and sweet and it is always a blast to be around my mom. We wanted to do a little hiking while we were in Moab on the way back to Idaho. There is an Arch on the side of the road that I say I want to hike every time I go through there but never do. Cory pulled over and I got so excited because we were going to walk up to the Arc.

The wind was blowing pretty hard and it was so cold. I was wearing shorts and a sweatshirt and Cory was wearing shorts and a jacket. When Cory got out of the car he was walking back and forth trying to find a spot to tie his shoes. Frustrated, I said, "Just pick a spot". We finally got under way and at the top we could see miles and miles of space. The Arc was so huge over our heads I thought how cool it would be to tie a swing around it.

There was one man on his way up to us and just before he got too close, Cory got down on one knee and asked me to marry him. As my tears fell, they kind of froze due to the weather but my heart was pounding really fast. It was truly a special moment. The gentleman made it up the hill to congratulate us then offered to take our picture. It was definitely a surprise and we were in no way dressed for a photo. I think those are the best ones in life. The unexpected moments with real emotions.

As we were going down the hill I apologized to Cory for the comment when he was acting like he was tying his shoe. He told me he was trying to get the ring in the right pocket and he almost changed his mind because of me. We just started laughing and I was yelling, "I'm engaged". I would apologize many more times in our relationship and he would throw in a couple from time to time. I continue to learn that not everyone needs to be on my schedule and do things the way I want even though their life would be better. I really believed that I knew best in most situations and I was going to help you whether you asked for it or not. Luckily, I continue to stay sober and am willing to learn, grow and change with every experience. I know what it is to be a good listener, communicator, co-worker and friend.

Chapter 49

Dakota was going to get married first. She and I went dress shopping and I was able to buy her the dresses she wanted. She went with a Bohemian style dress for her pictures and her wedding dress. I did what I needed to do to attend the ceremony in the temple. They had a reception at one of the local church buildings in Carlsbad. Dakota was stunning. Ian was very handsome as well. Cory and I had put a video together for Dakota of our lives up to that point. It makes me cry even today when I watch it. Making that video actually made it possible for Cory and I to marry a few months later.

A couple of times while we were dating, I tried to break up with Cory. I just wasn't sure I wanted to go down this path of marriage and now he wanted to join the church and go to the temple. That is a lot of pressure for a girl like me. When I broke up with people in the past, I did my best to stay friends. Cory made it very clear we would not be friends if we broke up. So, I broke up with him then went to his apartment the next day because he said he would help me with the video for Dakota. I learned later that he wanted to kick me out of his apartment and never see me again but his mentor said he had to keep his commitment to do the video. While doing the video I realized that God really wanted us to be together and I needed to get out my head and do the right thing and it would all work out.

Cory and I got our civil marriage in the church building where we attended then got sealed in the Salt Lake Temple. We didn't want a wedding and no reception was planned. We don't even celebrate our anniversary to this day. There is a part of me that wishes I had been in a financial situation where I could have had those things and the other part thinks the way we did it could be the best way to have a long marriage.

Here we have two people who were perfectly happy being single and had no plans for the future as far as a relationship, doing that exact thing. I did consider for a second having another baby but Cory was adamant that he didn't want to have kids and I felt relief in that. Just to be sure this wouldn't happen he got a vasectomy. I tried to talk him out of it in case we didn't work out but he assured me he didn't want them no matter what.

We decided not to consummate the marriage on the day of and actually didn't have a plan at all of when it would happen. Instead, we wanted it to just be random so we didn't let a piece of paper determine our sex life. Eventually it happened and all was good. It was strange being in this relationship sober and truly having someone I could talk to about anything and he could talk to me. When we get into disagreements it is generally me wanting something a certain way and him talking me out of it.

My Story

In recovery they talk about living beyond your wildest dreams and not leaving before the miracle. Early in recovery I had a friend who committed suicide when I lived in Idaho. A group of us ladies went to her house and did a project with her to get her more involved. She made everyone book markers with the 12 steps on them and passed them out at a women's retreat we all attended a few months before. When I got the call, I called Cory since he had more time than I did and I had no idea what to do or how to feel.

He told me to call my girlfriend Dawn. I called Dawn and she simply said, "This happens, and you have to continue living your life". Though it sounded harsh, I totally got it. I had planned to go to Rexburg that day to go down waterslides with Cory, Dakota and Ian.

I said a prayer for my friends and headed out. It was the most beautiful day. I think of my friend often and feel sad that she missed out on so much. People in recovery can be very matter of fact and we find humor in our tragedies. This is not only a survival skill but a life skill. This allows us to work with others in despair and give them the tools needed to move forward. No matter how difficult the task, the tools will get us through without a drink.

Chapter 50

Italy had been on my bucket list since I saw the movie "Under the Tuscan Sun". I wanted that exact movie to happen to me, well before I met Cory. Cory and I talked about going to Italy for a honeymoon. He took care of all travel arrangements, hotels and activities. We packed super light and researched what we should and shouldn't take with us. We landed in Rome and it was so dirty and the Colosseum was under renovation.

We walked forever trying to find the right place to eat while we were waiting for our hotel room to be available. We were exhausted from the flight and we had decided to stay up the whole day to try to get on track with the time change. This may sound miserable but it was amazing. We were together in a foreign country just winging it. I love this kind of stuff. I was supposed to learn the language but of course there were other more important things for me to do. Anything else but learning the language.

Finally Free

We finally got to our hotel and it was great. Our next stops would be Florence and Tuscany. We found a recovery meeting the first day in Rome and it was full of foreigners from all over the world. This was one of our favorite things to do. Go to meetings wherever we were visiting and take cookies. The meeting was awesome and we made some friends who we would see on our way back home.

Cory was getting annoyed with having to use the GPS and I said I would take the lead. He gave me our next stop and I just started walking. He let me walk for a little bit then yelled, "It's this way". My inability to find anything made him laugh and I just played it off because this will continue to be an issue for the rest of my life. In Florence we stayed in a hostel. Cory ate tons of gelato and we had some pretty decent food. We hiked the five cities and got to stay in a quaint hotel near a beach. There was so much salt in the water you could float even if you didn't know how to float.

In the small hallway upstairs next to our room, there was a tiny square window where you could look out and see the giant bell ringing. Cory pretty much had to duck in many places since he is 6'4". I had the best chocolate croissant in the village and when I ate it, I actually made an "mmm" sound. On our hike we walked through vineyards on the side of the mountain and we ate the grapes right off the vines.

We arrived in Tuscany and Cory found a beautiful hotel that was like something you see in the movies. He set up a couple's hot stone massage. I don't care for this type of massage because I want my muscles rubbed out, but no way was I going to complain. The massages were done by two women who enjoyed their smoke break while waiting for our rocks to cool down. She rubbed my face with her smokey little fingers. I was grateful that part didn't last very long.

When I saw the tiny thong underwear, I couldn't wait to talk to Cory about it afterwards. He was in another room so I had no idea what his experience would be. He said that he had put it on backwards and the lady had to tell him to turn it around. The way he tells a story always makes me laugh. He says don't let the truth ruin a good story. We then moved to the sauna and hot tub room. It had multiple of each and it was divine. Dinner was in the hotel restaurant which was just as fancy as the hotel. It was high enough to see all of Tuscany and the beautiful pool area. The food was perfect and after we finished eating, we were ready to hit the hay and prepare for our bike ride in the morning.

We showed up early at the bike shop and there were about 12 people in our group. We loaded into a large van and headed up to a wine tasting. This was part of the tour so we couldn't get out of it. It wasn't even hard to watch everyone sipping their wine in Tuscany which looks very different in the movies. It was hard waiting for them to finish. Drink it already, I thought. We have more to do. We got back on our bikes and headed to the highest hill I had ever ridden up. It was so steep people were dropping like flies and there were only four of us left. I knew that if I stopped peddling, I would not be able to get going again. I was standing straight up on my bike like I was walking. Cory was ahead of me doing awesome and giving me encouragement. We both made it to the top where we broke bread with the other guests sharing stories of where we were from and what brought us to Italy.

Chapter 51

We wanted to go to a huge waterfall that was within walking distance from the hotel. It turned out to be very far actually, but it was incredible once we got there. There were so many hot springs and so many people. One lady was walking around with no top on, just rolling around with the fast-running water. It was hilarious watching the men trying not to look at her and the women looking at the men. I thought, man I wish I was that brave. It looked like a lot of fun.

On our way back to the hotel it was incredibly hot. Since we had our bathing suits on, I told Cory we should jump into the pool. There was only one other guy in there so we jumped in. An older man came over tapping his head and yelling something at Cory. I told Cory that he probably wanted him to put a ponytail in his hair since it was long. Soon after another guy came with a cap for Cory to put on his head. It was black and white and he looked like he had on a condom. I have a great photo that I will always cherish and use against him as needed. At the hotel we were packing up to head back to Rome. I said to Cory in a dramatic British accent, "Don't take me back to the slums".

When we arrived in Rome, we went back to the same meeting we attended our first day in Italy. The guy leading the meeting remembered us and asked me to speak. We had no idea it was a speaker meeting and I only had about three years of sobriety. I shared my experience, strength and hope then the meeting was open for anyone to share. Cory decided he would go first. He said to the group, "I'm pissed off at her because she can't do anything right and you choose her to be a speaker". Everyone laughed. Cory then told me I was officially an international speaker which sounded really cool.

This planted a seed in me that one day I would go around the world and help people by sharing my story. We made it back to the States and life was going really well. I still struggled to accept that I was now married and living in Idaho and at times I felt the adventure was over. It took me two years of prayers to fully accept that I was married and everything was going to be okay. Sometimes I would talk to Cory about relationships not lasting and he told me, "I will stay with you even if I hate you". I certainly didn't want that to be a thing but it made me think of these people who have been married over 50 years. Is this what my first husband was thinking but couldn't express? Had I finally met my match, someone who wouldn't feed into my fleeing behaviors and unrealistic thinking? Had God really wanted me to have all of this?

The next year we bought a house with six bedrooms, a basement and a huge front and backyard. The neighborhood was mostly members of my church and great people. Ian and Dakota moved in with us so they could save money during school, which of course I loved. They stayed for a year and after graduating they decided to move to Texas. I decided to rent out the rooms and do the Airbnb thing. It was so much fun. We met people from all over, even Jerusalem.

We had a group of guys from Mexico stay with us while they were painting some apartments. One day we came home from church and they had the garage door open, playing loud Mexican music, grilling up carne asada and drinking beer. Cory and I busted up laughing. This neighborhood was not judgmental in any way but it was still odd to see this and it was coming from our house.

I was doing great at my job and in just 18 months I would qualify for a second retirement. So, of course, it was time to move. Cory had been researching places to live that were near beaches. He knew how much I loved the beach and that I would not be opposed to leaving Idaho to live near one. One night we were lying in bed and he asked me if I wanted to move to Hawaii. It was not foreign and we would not have to learn a new language. This was exactly what we needed to do. Become minimalists and move to an island.

We applied for jobs online and neither of us heard back from the employers. We decided to be proactive and take a trip there to speed up the process. We called our prospective employers and they agreed to give us interviews since we were going to be in town. How could they say no when we were taking the initiative to come so far? We were literally there for two sleeps. The interviews went well and we got the jobs.

Finally Free

When we got home Cory was sick for two weeks. This was the beginning of the Covid pandemic but it was not in full flight so we just thought he had the flu. My prospect kept pushing back the date until I convinced them we were ready to get to the island. Cory's job fell through due to Covid but we decided to go anyway. There are times when you fight for what you want and it is a good thing while other times when you push too hard it may not have been what God intended. I never could tell which is which so I just stick with pushing until I make it happen and deal with the consequences.

Chapter 52

We started preparing for the trip. We had only been in our amazing house for two years so we had all new furniture that I would now have to sell. We got our things down to 26 tubs. We had agreed to be minimalists on the next part of our journey but it was much harder than we thought it would be. Cory sold 1200 records that he had collected over the years. He was definitely committed. Since his brother and parents didn't live too far away, he was able to store some things with them. I had to get rid of my things and actually it was kind of freeing.

Dakota had come for a visit since we would be moving so far away and it was very expensive to travel. We would probably only see each other two or three times a month which seemed very unrealistic considering our relationship. I knew this was going to be a challenge and, in my heart, I also knew I was not staying on the island for too long. Dakota is my heart and I just want to be part of every part of her life and available if she needs me.

Finally Free

After the visit she traveled home and just a little later she Face Timed me. Ian was on the call, which he had not done before, so I should have known something was up. She held up three pregnancy sticks with the lines showing positive. I started running through the house crying and screaming and ran downstairs to include Cory. The look on his face was not of joy as much as, "Holy Crap, we're not moving to Hawaii". But this was not the case.

My brain was on overdrive. We were heading to Hawaii and my first grandbaby was coming. I made the decision that it was time to cut the cord and give me and Dakota the opportunity to live our lives apart. I really wanted this for both of us. I knew it was going to be difficult but I also knew this could be a very important thing to do. We continued with our plan.

Chapter 53

We had to quarantine for 14 days and there was literally only one option of a place to stay within our price range. We found a lady who seemed pretty quirky on the phone but harmless. She offered to pick us up from the airport because our car wouldn't be there for two more weeks after our arrival. Our 26 tubs were also on a boat floating towards the island. She showed up with two beautiful leis and put them around our necks.

She was very talkative and appeared to be someone who could benefit from a recovery program. She gave us a quick tour and was very adamant about us not leaving for any reason because she could get in trouble. We agreed. She lived way up on a hill on the Big Island, where everything is uphill; it's a volcano after all. We pulled into her driveway which meant we were not going to be able to park our own car because her tree dropped things on the cars that can ruin the paint.

Finally Free

We got out of the car and she led us to this room that was once part of a garage. It was about 400 square feet. It had white tile cabinets and a white tile floor. She had done the work herself and it showed. There were ants everywhere and a roach came to welcome us. She had been using the space for gardening and when we were coming, she quickly fixed it up. The bed was the first thing you ran into and to the left was the sink and the toilet right next to it. On the back wall beyond the bed was the shower. She was excited to show us the new red light she put in that changed colors. We were so exhausted we thanked her and didn't say a word. It took about 30 more minutes for her to leave.

She lived right upstairs and it was impossible to go outside without her knowing it. Sometimes I wondered if she had cameras but it was just the old screen on the door. She grew marijuana in her backyard for medicinal purposes which is why she didn't want any unexpected visitors. She loved gardening and I would never see her hands clean during the time I was there. I started doing work in her yard for her and because I couldn't go anywhere for 14 days. Cory just stayed inside and worked on his grateful dead show called "Official Tapes".

She talked constantly and sometimes I would comment but mostly I just let her talk. She was more excited for us to be there than I was to be in this room. We were in Hawaii and in 14 days we would see the island. When our 14 days were up, our car was still not there yet. I had talked to my mentor, Jennifer, and she gave me a number of her friend who lived on the island and was also in recovery. I called her and she offered to let us borrow one of her cars. Cory was able to meet with the program director of the station and they gave him

My Story

a part time gig that he could do from home. Later he found a job at an insurance company and became an insurance man.

My job started two days after quarantine. Luckily our Jeep got there the third day and we were able to pick it up on the other side of the island before the next full work week. As we drove around the island it was pretty incredible. I can honestly say there was no traffic. Moving in the middle of a pandemic has its benefits. The island took precautions from the very beginning which kept their numbers low for a very long time. We went to a beach called Magic Sands almost five days a week. No parking issues, no crowds. We couldn't go to any shops or restaurants because they were all closed. We got a Costco card and bought very little since we had no space to store it. When our things came, we were able to put them in the garage of the lady whose house we had quarantined in, which she offered before we came. Once the items were in there, she complained so the next day we went and bought a storage unit. After all, I had gotten used to these types of circumstances when living in other people's homes. We only had to stay in this room for three months. We needed to get a few paychecks coming in before we made a commitment to someplace with a year lease.

Chapter 54

I reached out to a couple I found on a local Facebook group. They wanted first and last which was $3600 and another $1500 for a deposit. Due to Covid prices shot up higher than usual because people were not paying their bills anymore since they weren't working so trust was a huge issue. Luckily, we had savings and were able to get into a one-bedroom condo. It was in a community where some residents were living full time and for others it was a second home. I did some networking at the pool and found good places to go that were still open and things to do. Most of the people living here were drinkers and retired so we had to find a meeting ASAP. It was seriously like we were stranded with a few other people making the best of it. We loved it but I missed Dakota very much. Since she had moved to Texas, I had to accept I wouldn't see her that often and I was never going to move to Texas.

Recovery was active on the island when we came for the initial visit but now it was mostly through Zoom due to the pandemic.

Finally Free

We came across a meeting right up the road from our condo. There were only three people and that was all we needed. We continued to go and the meeting continued to grow as the number of Covid deaths declined.

The beach meetings started opening up which were really fun. The only problem was the waves were so loud you could only hear the person talk if they were right next to you. That was okay with me because the vibe from the waves gave me what I needed for the day. It was just a strange time in the world and people were closed off. I felt like we were just going to the meeting to keep up our program and stay connected but were really connecting to the people in the meeting. I was missing Idaho very much.

We found our routine and went on some beautiful hikes. I skated along the beach and walked the hills daily. Sometimes I would run along the beach but when I got to the sand area I tended to stop and put my feet in the ocean. Bike riding was tough due to all of the hills and like on the mainland cars weren't fans of cyclists. On the highway it was okay but the wind would be so strong it made it less fun. This island was not like Oahu or Kauai. You had to search for sandy beaches and there was always a down side. The beach in Waikoloa was perfect except the wind blew sand in your face so hard it wasn't fun to lay out or read a book. On the Hilo side it rained often and the water could get chilly. These are called "Cadillac problems". Complaining about things like wind or hills when you live on an island and can see the ocean no matter where you are.

Cory found an amazing hike that was 15 hours long and we camped at the beach below the night before so we could get up early the next morning and head up. It was Christmas and someone was letting off M-80s. We were in a canyon so it sounded like we were getting bombed. This went on until two or three in the morning. With little sleep we packed everything up and secured the Jeep. We had to walk through some treacherous rocks and water to get to the other side of the beach to begin the hike.

The path up the volcano was very thin and straight up. There were many sharp rocks so we had to keep our heads down and remind ourselves to look up to enjoy the view once in a while. The water was so blue and the sand was a blackish grey. The first part of the climb was on the face of the rock. Eventually we made our way into a jungle area. It was muggy and there were so many mosquitos it was impossible to swat them away. We had to move quickly before we no longer had any blood left in our bodies. We were six hours in and the sun would be setting in four. It was time to turn around so we could be at the bottom before dark. We made it back to watch the sunset on the beach on Christmas Day 2020 in Hawaii.

Chapter 55

Living on the island was like *Ground Hog Day*. The same day over and over. It was beautiful but everything was expected; there are no surprises. Until April 6th, Good Friday 2021. I had an appointment with my doctor to discuss getting surgery on my shoulder. My appointment was later in the day so I thought I would go roller skating to pass the time. My friend Ron and I tried to get a group of people together but we were the only two who showed up.

We headed out and, on the way back to our cars, my skate hit a small rock which sent my wheels into a crack and I fell the wrong direction trying to protect my shoulder. I heard a snap and had instant pain. I just said, "No, No, No". I had never broken or sprained anything in my life so I knew this was bad. I told Ron to get my skate off quickly. When he pulled it off, I was holding my shin and my foot separated from my ankle and went to the ground.

Finally Free

I wanted to cry so bad but the pain was intense and I was trying to hold it in so many different ways so the pain would just stop. We were too far from our vehicles but a lady who was walking wanted to call an ambulance while another lady wanted to give us a ride. Ron quickly said, "No, an ambulance will take too long and it's too expensive". Even in the pain I was in I really appreciated him saying that. Ron and the lady picked me up while I was holding my ankle and foot together. The pain just wouldn't stop, I seriously couldn't believe how badly it hurt and there was no angle to ease the pain. I can't even describe or give it a number. I just knew my tolerance level was at zero.

This was where the shit show began. Covid was in full force by this time, we had been masked up since we moved here and that rule never went away. There were more people on the island due to the safe travel methods that were in place which made it difficult to get good service. We pulled up to the hospital and the lady who drove me went in to get someone to get me out of the car. Two girls in scrubs came up to the vehicle asking me questions while I was holding my foot and ankle together. Ron arrived at this time and was exchanging numbers with the lady who drove me. The two girls told me they had to see whether someone could see me right now and if not, the ER would come pick me up and take me back to another hospital. I had no idea the ER was on the other side of Kona. After what felt like an hour, they finally came back and wheeled me into an X-Ray. I had a fractured fibula, a chipped tibia and possible torn tendons.

Chapter 56

They didn't know about the torn tendons until the day of surgery. The PA gave me a shot to numb the pain. This shot was worse than the pain I already had and I begged him to pull it out. Then it started working and I could breathe. They wrapped it up and sent me home. I could not go get surgery for four days because they didn't do Covid testing on the weekends. I had to travel to Oahu for the surgery and back home the same day. No one told my husband that I was ready to go so I waited for a couple hours before he came back for me since he couldn't wait in the hospital. I found this out later or I would have called him.

When the surgeon told me I was going to have a 12-week recovery I knew he meant it. But I didn't know that it was just from the surgery. It would take six months to a year for a full recovery. During Covid there was a lot of movement around the world. People were moving closer to family and we were going to join this group. My last three months in Hawaii were on crutches and it gave me a lot of time to think about what is really important to me. I made the best of my time but I knew it was time for me to get back to the mainland. Cory and I agreed to move to Texas even though neither of us wanted to go there. Before we left Dakota wanted to come visit for her birthday with the baby, so we could hang out at the beach.

I bought one of those bags to put over my leg and had a nice brace to protect my leg. It was horrible not being able to go in the water with Dakota and the baby, Hazel. They went hiking and had a great time exploring. I had made plans for us to go to a comedy show. Our neighbors Trish and Dewey watched the baby. They were a couple we had dinner with most Sundays. The show was okay but it made me think I could do that. I always wanted to try being a comedian and this would be the best place to do it. I was leaving so if I sucked it wouldn't matter. They had a competition coming up the following month. I told Dakota I was going to enter.

I had no idea how to prepare or what I was going to talk about. I received an email on things I was not allowed to talk about which was weird because I have heard comedians talk about pretty awful things and they make a lot of money. It did help me realize the world is so sensitive right now so I would stick to alcoholics and family. I got to the show and I was super nervous. I was still on crutches and I was so excited that I was finally going to do this. As soon as I got the microphone in my hand and heard the first laugh, I felt right at home. I ended up winning the competition and left the island as the "Funniest Person on the Big Island". This made me want to move even more because maybe I could go to other places on the mainland and do stand up.

My Story

I had to wait until my doctor released me to put weight on my leg and it felt like forever. The move off the island went with ease so we knew it was the right choice. I said goodbye to the small number of friends I made on the island and was ready to go home. Home, meaning the mainland, because we were going to have to start all over again finding a place to live, buying all the things, finding jobs, making friends, etc.

Chapter 57

We are now living in the best part of Texas and loving life. My ankle continues to heal and I am getting stronger every day. We found great recovery here in Austin. I have made awesome friends and have a workout partner, Tiesa, who shows up and we push through our workouts no matter how painful it will be the next day. We have a lot in common including the same type of car. This may sound simple, but in my recovery program, it's the little things that help me stay sober.

This journey thus far has shown me that I will continue to have challenges in my life and it is how I move through them that will give me what I need. Life isn't about getting what I want. It's about acceptance of what has been given to me from God, doing service for others, being grateful in all things, working hard and most of all, family.

I have a beautiful new grandbaby named Hazel who I literally get to be with every day. A son-in-law named Ian, who loves my girls with

Finally Free

all of who he is. Then there's my amazing daughter, Dakota, who will always be my number one and who I will cherish forever. There are truly no words to describe the love I have for Dakota. Finally, I have a husband who continues to encourage me and participate in my crazy adventures.

I have learned so much through writing this book and my goal is to inspire others to fight for their life, dream big and let the past make you stronger. Fear is an action and to move into freedom the requirement is the same. I am finally free of alcohol one day at a time and will continue to work with others in recovery and share my story so I can keep what God has so graciously given to me. Thank you for being a part of my journey. Cheers!

My Story

Finally Free

My Story

Finally Free

My Story

Afterword

The fun must continue! I'm scheduled for speaking engagements, book signings, and other events which are posted on my website - fianllyfreebook.com - and social media. I'll continue to plan and participate at workshops and retreats that inspire others to find their freedoms through meditation, health and fitness, mind-body-soul awareness, and communication activities.

My interest is helping others discover what is holding them back from accomplishing their goals. I walk with them through the hard stages in life so they find their personal freedom.

Change is possible and available! Come join me in this adventure. See you soon!

To schedule my service for an event please contact me at 808-747-6287 or foutzie44@yahoo.com
finallyfreebook.com

About the Author

Carol Foutz was born in Los Angeles California and spent most of her school age years in New Mexico. She was named the Funniest Person on The Big Island in Hawaii, 2021. Carol has a Master's Degree in School Counseling and a Bachelors in Education. Carol, is passionate about her family and working with diverse youth. Finally Free is her first book and she is welcoming all into her journey of resilience, fear, heart break, and growth through adventures beyond her wildest dreams.

Email: foutzie44@yahoo.com
Website: finallyfreebook.com

Carol Foutz

Carol was named the funniest person on the big Island Hawaii in 2021. Her comedic outlook inspired the humor in her tragedies and encouraged continual change throughout her story. Born in Los Angeles, California, Carol has earned a BS and MS, and has always been into fitness. She was named the officer of the year while working in corrections and her passion is helping people.

Carol has an innate ability to communicate with people with compassion and understanding, making it possible to build trusting relationships. She learned early in life to be self-motivated and encouraging to others to be positive and not make excuses to achieving her goals.

Through her speaking, Carol will inspire others to recognize their strengths and discover the truth behind what holds people back from seeing the value that already exists inside them.

Speaking Topics:

Communication
Listening is the best action in communicating. Receiving information will encourage change.

Be about it
Talking about change is exhausting. Change in motion is motivating and inspiring. Let's stop just talking, and get moving.

Did you really let it go?
How do we let go and what do we keep to strengthen our body, mind and soul?

Simplifying your relationship with money

✉ foutzie44@yahoo.com   🔗 finallyfreebook.com

Notes

www.ingramcontent.com/pod-product-compliance
Lightning Source LLC
Chambersburg PA
CBHW021435080526
44588CB00009B/531